No
Foothold
in the
Swamp

CHARLES
HOLLINGSWORTH

No Foothold in the Swamp

A Story of One Man's Burnout in the Ministry

Ministry Resources Library

Zondervan Publishing House • Grand Rapids, MI

Ministry Resources Library is an imprint of Zondervan Publishing House, 1415 Lake Drive, S.E., Grand Rapids, Michigan 49506.

Library of Congress Cataloging in Publication Data

Hollingsworth, Charles E.
    No foothold in the swamp.

    Bibliography: p.
    I. Title.
PS3558.034976N6   1988   813'.54   88-5329
ISBN 0-310-31770-3

Edited by Michael G. Smith

Printed in the United States of America

88 89 90 91 92 93 / AH / 10 9 8 7 6 5 4 3 2 1

To my beloved wife,
who means more to me than words can tell.
Also, to my bishop,
my pastor, friend, and father in God.

Acknowledgments

I am grateful to have an opportunity to tell this tale. During the earliest days of my conscious commitment to Christ I was taught that the Lord wastes no experiences. I have borne this principle in mind while writing this book. I pray that these words will enable clergy and laity to avoid the misery that engulfed me, my family, and our congregation.

During the past few years many people have played a part in bringing this little volume to birth, and I wish to thank them. First and foremost, I am grateful to my wife. She is indeed "worth far more than rubies" (Prov. 31:10). Without her love and loyalty my misery would have been deeper. She has both encouraged and creatively criticized this work from beginning to end.

In our time of trial an ecumenical cross section of colleagues stood by us, as did a fine physician and a gifted therapist. That my bishop never lost confidence in me did more than anything else to keep me from tumbling into oblivion. We owe you all a debt of gratitude.

Finally, I wish to thank Zondervan editor Michael Smith for his insights and gentle treatment of a manuscript that has become as much a part of my family as my children, the cat, and the dog!

Contents

Save me, O God,
    for the waters have come up to my neck.
I sink in the miry depths,
    where there is no foothold.
I have come into the deep waters;
    the floods engulf me.
I am worn out calling for help;
    my throat is parched.
My eyes fail,
    looking for my God.

(Ps. 69:1–3, JB)

Preface

A few years ago my ministry almost came to an explosively premature end when I began sinking into the mire and discovered that I had burned out. It was a terrifying nightmare, and I will always bear scars of the psychological and spiritual torment through which I passed.

My whole family journeyed through a dark and fearsome valley and was nearly destroyed. We emerged chastened yet refined. What we experienced was a constant reminder to the one who stands: Beware lest ye fall. By God's grace we are richer and more tolerant people.

Out of that journey came this novel. The main character, Jeremy Wilkinson, is partly me, but he also bears a striking resemblance to half a dozen colleagues, Catholic and Protestant. All of us burned out. Some have recovered, but others are lost to the ordained ministry forever. The setting and the characters are an amalgam. Any similarity to particular places and persons is purely circumstantial.

I have set my tale within the Episcopal church because that is the one I know best. But this story could be told in the trappings of any ecclesiastical setting. Jeremy Wilkinson's plight afflicts women and men wherever they pour themselves out in the service of God. Burnout in the ministry happens more frequently than most of us care to admit.

I want you to identify with Jeremy as he plunges into an agonizing voyage of self-discovery. When he hurts, try to feel his pain; as he finds the building blocks of recovery and experiences anew the loving-kindness of our God, rejoice with him.

When a minister burns out, the accompanying spiritual

9

and emotional unraveling so frighten congregations that the sufferer is often forced out of his/her pastorate—rapidly.

"The church is the only organization that shoots its wounded" are words I have heard too often. I am eternally grateful to be part of a tradition that does not abandon sufferers to their own devices. As you read this story, I hope you will see ways to support individuals who are wrestling with demons because of their vocational commitment to Jesus Christ.

I present this book not as an intellectual exercise or for amusement or spiritual titillation, but so that you may gain insights that can then be used in your life or the lives of your fellow clergy or in the life of the one who ministers in your congregation.

There are no easy answers to the complex problems that burnout raises. Whether you or someone close to you is the victim of this plight, please be tolerant, asking always that God will bring resurrection from the mess with which you are trying to cope. There is life—abundant life—beyond burnout!

1

We sat there looking at one another as we had done on so many occasions over the last year or so. The late summer sun slanted through the window, and a mellowness in the breeze hinted that autumn was at hand.

Jonathan smiled. "How are you doing, then?"

"When are you going to learn a different opener than that for a counseling session?" I replied, grinning as I taunted him. Over the many months in which we had delved into the hidden recesses of my life, we had developed a fast friendship that allowed me to call his bluff.

It was his turn to grin. He sat there like the Cheshire cat in *Alice*, his head cocked to one side, his eyes sparkling. We remained silent together, enjoying a closeness of companionship that is seldom possible for two men alone together in a state of wordlessness.

I first entered Jonathan's inner sanctum well over a year ago. My desire to seek counseling had startled those whom I had told, for they did not know the turmoil that had been ripping me to shreds for so long. Like most pastors, I had learned to pretend and could put on the mask of the imperturbable professional carer so well that sometimes I was not even aware of the great storms that blew across the features of my own psyche.

But that summer a series of events had accelerated a process of decline that had been taking place for a very long time. Picking up the telephone and calling Jonathan was the only way I could hope to retain my sanity. One Sunday morning at the conclusion of the service, I was scared out of my wits by the thought that I might be going mad. A month or two later I found myself walking with a friend and wondering aloud whether God even existed. If he did, then he was showing very little interest in me and my problems.

Now, thirteen months later, Jonathan and I sat in our accustomed places looking at each other and wondering who would be the first to break the silence. We had played this game before, and Jonathan usually won. When I had been working as rector of a church, I had occasionally tried this trick with people who came to see me. On those occasions I usually won. Although Jonathan was, like me, an Episcopal priest, he was a trained psychologist and counselor. He was far better suited to this sort of exercise than I was.

*   *   *

Before I go on, I should introduce myself. My name is Jeremy Wilkinson. I am forty-four years old and have spent most of my adult life working as an Episcopal priest in parishes in various parts of the country, most recently in New England. The story I have to tell is one that may frighten some of my readers, for it describes the devastating effects of what has become known as "ministerial burnout" on a man whom many expected to do something significant for God in the Episcopal church. That promising man is me.

The tale I tell is messy and, unlike the stories that are packaged into sixty-minute episodes for television, it has no ending. I will describe for you my pilgrimage to date, because like every autobiography, the story has yet to conclude. I will be as candid and probing as I can, because what happened to me is occurring in the lives of pastors everywhere, every day. Few people, clergy or laity, realize how unyieldingly stressful the ordained ministry is. Most of us underestimate the effects that long periods of pressure can have on the men and women who serve God on the front line—in the parishes.

If you are a member of the clergy, you may know the feeling of rising anger that you have to curtail when a parishioner jokingly suggests that you work only one day a week. If you are a layperson, you may find yourself wondering from time to time why your pastor looks, sounds, and behaves as if he is at the end of his tether. Let me tell you, the ordained life can kill and maim. The more capable or conscientious your pastor is, the more likely a candidate he or she is for ministerial burnout.

Impending burnout took me to Jonathan's office. If it had not been for him, my bishop, and a handful of loving friends, I do not know where I would be today. I am not the suicidal type, but even if I had not taken my own life at that point, I might still have committed some other kind of spiritual or emotional hari-kari.

*   *   *

A multitude of thoughts tumbled through my mind as Jonathan and I sat there staring at each other and waiting for the silence to be broken. He picked up his pipe, expertly stuffed tobacco into its bowl, struck a match, and puffed meditatively until the bluish smoke danced in the rays of soft light that angled through the windows into the room and shimmered on the dust hanging in the air.

At last I spoke. "You know, Johnny, I think the time has come for me to take a rest from this counseling business. We demolished and reconstructed me pretty well. My checkbook is screaming for relief. But I'm certain I will be back. Counseling is like exercising—you have to keep at it if you are to remain psychologically fit."

"I'm glad to hear you say that, Jeremy; I was thinking along those lines as well. We have come a long way, haven't we?"

I chuckled. "You bet. And I didn't know there was so much dirt stuck in the tangled entrails in my life."

"You know now, my friend."

"And by the grace of God, I won't forget it in a hurry."

We smiled at each other, and a peacefulness descended over the room again. The only sounds that could be heard were the rustle of the leaves outside the open window and the distant muffled sound of traffic in the street.

"What are you thinking?" Jonathan asked. This was a regular ploy that he used to delve into a client's thought world, and I might add, it was a very successful one.

"Oh, I was just thinking about the sad state I was in when I first started coming to see you."

"Uh, huh," he nodded.

"I guess I was not at my worst, but I was going downhill pretty rapidly. You intimated in your initial diagnosis that I might be experiencing some sort of emotional hiccup, if I remember correctly. If I had let you into the deepest recesses of my being there and then, your attitude might have been very different. When I first arrived in this room I was determined to keep some of myself to myself."

"That's hardly surprising. It takes time for people to soften up and start baring their souls to someone who is more or less a stranger. Some folk who come in here couldn't even do it if they tried. They are so locked up in themselves that their defenses are virtually impossible to break through."

I spoke again. "At the beginning there was a great deal about myself that I did not want you to know. I thought I could give you the information in a censored form. Then you would do the impossible and make sense of my situation, working with only a fragment of the picture. Months passed before we began getting down to the real business of discovering who I was, because it took so long for me to feel at ease enough to pour it all out, good and bad."

My counselor relit his pipe and nodded again.

* * *

I remember well that first afternoon I went to see Jonathan. As I drove to his office I was sweating profusely. At the time I was wondering whether it might not be worth having air-conditioning put into my car, for I was raised in the snowbelt and have never found the summer's heat easy to handle.

14

The perspiration was not simply a natural reaction to the heat; it was also brought on by fear. I was going to allow someone else to delve into my innermost life and feelings. Although I am ostensibly a very open person, like everyone else I have a part of me that I want to keep private. In that private person I covered the blackness that Jonathan was eventually to begin uncovering. Perhaps I realized even then that I would not be able to hide from his gentle inquisition forever.

Sitting there waiting for his previous appointment to conclude, I felt self-conscious. Should I make idle conversation with the secretary-receptionist? Should I have worn my clerical collar? Should I take a cup of coffee? I felt like a boy waiting to see the principal on his first day at a new school. Here I was—a member of the clergy seeking the support and help of a psychologist. Somehow it seemed wrong, an admission of failure on my part, even if the counselor was ordained too.

My stomach was in turmoil. The butterflies had been having a ball for months. Despite the more relaxed summer schedule at church, I felt tense and edgy. My appetite had been ebbing away for a long time. Although I always eat less when it is hot, by that point I was not consuming enough to keep a gnat, let alone a grown man, alive.

I knew that I had lost more weight than was good for me. I could not do the "Special K pinch" that the cereal commercials were always blabbing about. In my case there had never been the need to diet; I had always had that lean and hungry look. If Jonathan could help me this afternoon, I would be eating normally in no time. But many months were to pass before I started putting on a few pounds again.

Jonathan and I had known each other for years. We had met at clergy gatherings and Episcopal jamborees where we had casually passed the time of day. When I first arrived on Boston's North Shore I had been leery of him, not knowing precisely what to make of a priest whose ministry was counseling. I heard mixed reports of his abilities, some swearing by his capacity to bring emotional healing, others

15

not sure he did anything but listen and take a large fee at the close of the counseling hour.

I went to see Jonathan, however, because he had been in parish ministry for a number of years. From his own experience and a long practice of working with others in positions similar to mine, he was better equipped than anyone else I knew to prevent me from drowning in my own misery.

The door of Jonathan's inner sanctum opened, and a high-strung, fashionably dressed woman in her thirties stepped out and disappeared down the hallway. Jonathan followed her, smiling as he walked past me to see her to the front door. As he breezed by he asked me to go right in and make myself at home.

I tried to be casual as I sat down on the faded, long green sofa that dominated the room. On the wall in front of me was a print depicting an open window through which a winding pathway stretching across fields of grass toward some woods on the distant horizon could be seen. Obviously a wind was blowing, because some tattered net curtains were billowing into the room toward the place where the artist was situated.

"How relaxing a view," I thought, but I did not have time to explore the composition in depth, for Jonathan returned at that moment, and we started talking.

In the weeks and months that followed, I gazed into the distance of that picture so many times that it will be etched upon my memory until the day I die. Every time I looked at it I wondered what was beyond the line of trees: a meadow perhaps, or even the ocean? "Lord," I would pray on those days when I thought I could believe in him, "make it be the ocean."

As I sat there waiting I knew there still might be time for me to escape while he was using the bathroom. The temptation was great, but I restrained myself. A troubled person, unless he is a fool, no more turns his back on the only help available than a drowning man refuses to cling to a life preserver. But just my being there sorely wounded my pride.

"Perhaps it is my pride, my overweening ego, that has

prevented me from asking for assistance until now," I mused. "Jonathan's a good man, and I know I can trust him, but it sure feels funny sitting here." Waiting for the counselor to return, I discovered the sinking sensation in the pit of the stomach that a prisoner experiences while waiting for the judge to pass sentence upon him.

These ponderings got no further, for suddenly Jonathan was there in front of me perusing the clipboard containing the information blank that I had completed while waiting outside his office door. He sat down and smiled sympathetically.

"Well, my friend, what brings you here today?"

As I have mentioned already, I had promised myself that I would not tell the man everything. There were certain areas of my life that I felt should be off-limits—even to his probings. Negotiating my way through the afternoon traffic I had composed a little speech with which I would begin: I wanted to be in the driver's seat.

As far as I was concerned, a few weeks spent bouncing ideas off this fellow would be enough to straighten out the bent bumpers and dented fenders of my life and head me in the right direction again. How foolish an assumption this was. How badly I had underestimated the agony of the experiences through which I had been passing and the damage that I had done to myself.

"Well, Jonathan, I haven't been doing too well lately. My nerves are on edge, I've lost my appetite, and various things have gone wrong, bringing to the surface a lot of junk that I think needs clearing away so that I can get on with my life and ministry."

He nodded, encouraging me to carry on.

Slowly the story of the previous months began to unwind. Of course at that point it was the expurgated version: the deepening sense of depression; constant tiredness, now coupled with an inability to sleep properly; a sense of loneliness, heightened by the fact that having spent a number of weeks earlier in the year traveling round the country on a national church commission, I did not feel able to leave the parish for a long period so soon. Therefore, my wife had taken

17

our children to see her folks by herself for a good portion of the summer.

What I did not tell Jonathan was that I needed a break from my wife for a while. Not only had I overestimated my ability to bounce back after an exhausting year, I had also had my fill of the pesterings of the woman I had married when we were fresh out of college.

During this first session we talked in general terms about my misgivings about parish ministry, a creeping malaise that had left me wondering whether I could continue in this job for the remainder of my working life. When we got to talking about my marriage I suggested that the relationship had taken quite a battering over the last seven or eight years, but I did not tell him how sick to death we had become of each other.

When the hour was over we stood up.

"What's wrong with me?" I asked.

"Nothing that a little talking will not help you resolve. You have a bit of a vocational struggle going on, and your marriage could do with some sprucing up."

"Yes, I suppose Rachel and I have become a bit of a habit with one another, but that's not particularly unusual when you've been married fourteen or fifteen years, is it?"

Jonathan did not reply. Ever since then I have rerun the concluding moments of that session through my head and puzzled over whether he was deliberately understating the magnitude of our problems. Or had I given him so little information about the real state of affairs that he was unable to see beyond what I had said? My instinct tells me that he was understanding the situation and did not want to alarm me too much. However, I do not always trust instincts.

We set another date, and I walked out into the sunshine. There was a lightness in my gait that had been missing for weeks.

"This is a piece of cake," I thought. "I can't understand the fuss people make about the pain of counseling or the stupid forebodings I had before we got started."

2

The forebodings I harbored before my first counseling session had been quelled by Jonathan's gentle manner, but my fears had not been groundless. How adamantly I repeated to myself that I would not tell him any more than I felt necessary. I am sure that the main reason for my negativity was that I was terrified by the abyss that seemed to be opening up beneath me.

If I had kept the door to my private self closed, I would not have benefited from the therapy I was being offered. But Jonathan had all the patience in the world and soon had a handle on what I was up to. He bided his time until my pain became so acute that I could no longer smother the secret agonies of my heart.

Gradually, almost imperceptibly, our sessions changed from urbane conversations that walked around the perimeter of my troubles into emotionally grueling skirmishes that attempted to break down the barriers I had thrown up to guard the deep recesses of my troubled life. There were times when I found myself hating Jonathan for all that he was discovering about me. He was driving a coach and horses through the emotional wall I had built around myself during my years of ministry. Sometimes it was all I could do to drag myself to his office, so unwilling was I to psychologically strip myself in his presence.

But I *would* go. There was a cauldron boiling deep within me, and the only way I could let off steam was by sitting on that long green sofa, staring at that picture, spilling out my anger, confusions, bitterness, and bewilderment. Meanwhile that lovely man would sit there puffing on a Sherlock Holmes style pipe and encouraging me along with occasional comments or penetrating questions.

As the months passed, glimmers would appear at the end of the tunnel. Some would fade, but some became shining, glowing lights that helped to make sense of the wilderness through which I was journeying. Bit by bit I discovered parts of myself that had lain buried for as long as I could remember. Corpses from the past needed to be exhumed, examined, and then either resurrected or given a decent Christian burial.

There are times when counseling is like confession. Indeed, on at least one occasion I found it necessary to make sacramental confession to Jonathan, who in his role as a priest of the Episcopal church pronounced absolution over me in the name of Jesus Christ. Not everyone would find that helpful, but I did.

What had I said to myself as I left that first counseling session? "This is a piece of cake. I can't understand the fuss people make about the pain of counseling." How mistaken I was. From my present perspective I chuckle at my naïveté. Anyone who has gotten into the state I was in before reaching out and asking for help will likely agree that counseling can sometimes turn into emotional surgery—without benefit of anesthetic. From the deep recesses of your inner being demons appear that appall you, but once they have been exorcised, as in Christ's parable of the demons, the vacuum has to be filled, and the counselee is not sure how to fill it.

Exorcism is not a simple laying on of hands accompanied by fervent prayer. It can be long, draining, and uncertain. In my case I was up to my chin and about to drown before the tide began to turn. When I was a boy and began to move into Christian circles, one of the first messages I imbibed was that Christians do *not* get angry. Very early in my counseling I learned how angry a person I am and how much I had bottled up for so long. But from my adolescence on I had virulently denied this aspect of my personality. Instead of

20

venting my feelings, I would repress them. This did me no good whatsoever.

I tend to feel everything passionately: I love passionately and I hate passionately. Although my style in the pulpit is fairly restrained, beneath the surface is a glowing furnace. Over the years, I have committed myself to all sorts of causes with singular fervor. Deep within me is a yearning to see justice and truth triumph. When this does not happen I get livid. Unfortunately, I tend to be too good-mannered and have kept my passionate nature on a short leash.

This bottling-up of my being became a habit so that few people, except my wife, ever noticed. People looking at the controlled and restrained me simply assumed that they were seeing the real me. Of course they weren't. The real me was angry and imprisoned in the inmost heart of my psyche. As certain as sunrise I was setting a trap for myself into which I would fall during my late thirties. It was as if I were filling a tub of boiling oil into which I would throw myself when I could no longer hold my feelings in.

Along with my anger, there were other parts of me that were being submerged: my sexuality, my sense of humor, my innate creativity—the list is endless. In one way or another I connived to lose my own identity behind the genteel mask of Jeremy Wilkinson, dedicated priest and pastor.

But it is impossible to deny one's true self forever. During those first few months of therapy I was forced to face not only elements of my personality that had become submerged but also the darker side of my soul. Then suddenly I was up close looking at my maggot-ridden interior through the strong lens of a magnifying glass.

*   *   *

During that wrap-up counseling session over two years later Jonathan asked me whether I could enumerate some of the facts I had learned about myself. The one I dwelled upon longest was my anger.

"Well," I began, "I suppose I've discovered it is not

contrary to Christian faith to be uncontrollably angry at times. For so long I had so much anger pent up within me that I didn't know what to do with it. I guess I turned it all in on myself. Then the more I looked at myself, the less I liked what I saw."

Jonathan nodded. I couldn't tell what sort of nod it was: sometimes I could figure out a nod that meant he agreed; at other times it was a nod of assent to assure me that he was still listening. By this stage in our relationship I could interpret his nods pretty well, but on this occasion I was not sure.

I continued talking. "I came to you feeling at sea with my life and depressed beyond all reason. While there was a multitude of reasons for the way I felt, that I had never allowed my anger an opportunity to vent itself must have played a significant part in my story."

This time he nodded vigorously, and I knew that he not only agreed but was telling me I was headed in the right direction.

"Looking back over the last couple of years I would say that you gave me permission to get cross from time to time—to raise my voice, to holler and scream. Indeed, I remember very early on in this odyssey having a fascinating conversation with Phil Harper. You know the guy I mean—that Congregational minister who's so much larger than life and runs that rather offbeat counseling practice down in Arlington."

Jonathan muttered something and then allowed me to continue. "He was into primal scream therapy at the time and was convinced that it is extremely healthy for us to scream and yell. Such screaming lets more oxygen into the brain and leads to mental health—or at least that's the theory. I found it convincing at the time, but I couldn't say whether it's true or not. What I do know is that I feel much better those days when I have had an opportunity to ventilate when a mishap occurs or when someone has trampled across my toes."

Pictures of occasions when my shell of urbane sophistication had begun to crack raced through my brain—when I had become angry with a colleague or with my children, but particularly those occasions when my wife had taken me to the end of my rope. As counseling went on, those events became more and more frequent. There was nothing I wanted to do more most of the time than to knock the woman into the middle of next week.

It is too early in my story to start telling you about my marriage. Suffice it to say that in the midst of many of the difficulties was a deepening animosity toward the woman to whom I had been married for so many years. We had problems in our relationship that we had walked around for far too long. With Rachel the little niggles that any husband has about his wife had multiplied. Yet I had ignored them, pretending this was the best way to love her.

Perhaps the hardest fact for me to confront honestly was that over the years I had found myself toying with the idea that I no longer loved my wife. I was relieved when I was not in her company, . . . but I'm allowing myself to race ahead of my story.

The expression of open anger in our marriage arrived like a volcanic eruption that could challenge the performance of Mount St. Helens or even Krakatoa! We had been so polite for so long that that boringly predictable pattern of interaction was suddenly shattered. Now each of us was forced to step out of the roles we had created, and all hell seemed to break loose!

I did not feel angry toward my wife alone; I was mad at my parish, my bishop, and my family. I took aim at anything that was in sight. Sometimes I would walk the beach yelling bloody murder into the deafening roar of the Atlantic breakers as they surged up the sand, buffeted by cold winter winds. The wildness of a dark, windy, rainswept beach perfectly reflected the turmoil of my soul.

At other times I would sit at home and brood over the hateful thoughts that floated to the top of my brain and over which I seemed to have little control. I would talk for hours with anyone who would listen to me, ranting and raving about the unfairness of life and how dreadful everything was. Alice was one such person. She was a widow in my congregation who had silently watched my struggle over several years and had shrewdly concluded that something was dreadfully wrong. Becoming aware of her concern, I began confiding in her until she knew my life history not only inside out but also upside down.

My first autumn in counseling was crisp and golden: New England at its best. Playing hooky from the office, Alice and I would walk the seashore, through the woods, or around the many ponds in that part of Massachusetts. She would listen quietly as I dumped on her the knotted jumble of thoughts that writhed and twisted through my mind. Most of them were unsavory, and my language was richly marinated in vitriol.

"Where has all this viciousness come from?" I would cry in my despair. "How could it be that an apparently loving parish priest could allow such a thing to happen to him?"

I wondered whether the Devil had taken control of my life. However, at that very moment I was having trouble believing in God, so the notion of an Evil One stretched my credulity beyond its limits. In subtle ways perhaps he had, but I am not sure the moment of possession was that recent.

It may have come when I became enmeshed in a Christian tradition that did not give its followers an opportunity to express their negative feelings. I went through my formative teenage years cultivating a calm exterior while denying the fierce battle that was being fought inside. Christ had chased the money changers from the court of the temple in Jerusalem, but we have always found ways to explain away his anger.

From this perspective in time I am beginning to think that at least I was trying to escape from the Devil's bondage. As I did so, other parts of my personality started fragmenting and falling to pieces. I began to wind down. I would sit in my office for hours staring at nothing, seeing nothing, and achieving less.

Like an overloaded computer, the systems of my brain were

sequentially shutting down, and I was incapable of doing anything about it. Frankly, I did not want to do anything about it. For what seemed like an eternity, I had worked myself into the ground, and now I needed to take a rest—a long, long rest. If I had my druthers, I never wanted to work again, certainly not as a pastor.

The dreams that filled my mind were visions of a totally secular existence—no parish, no clerical collar chafing my neck, no expectations being laid upon me. I thought of how wonderful it would be to never enter a church again; to have Sundays to myself; to not have to preach or celebrate the Eucharist for the remainder of my life; to do all those things that had been forbidden me.

I knew I could be as lusty as the next guy, and I could be the life and soul of the party if I tried. I longed for the opportunity to shed the mantle of clerical respectability that had clothed me for most of my working life and to let go of my inhibitions. Why shouldn't I? Since the Christian message was making little sense to me, perhaps the wisest course of action would be to make a complete break with this whole charade of faith and morals, resign my orders, and feast on the forbidden fruit of a faithless world.

3

Although several years have passed since the events I have related to you engulfed me, I am still shaken by the violence of my reaction to them. At the time, it seemed that my primary goal was to destroy myself and those around me, yet as I attempt to examine my motives, nothing could be further from the truth.

While the nightmare lasted, my perceptions became so twisted that I thought I was creating something new and beautiful. I reasoned that the agony I was experiencing was due to my attempts to build a new future on the crumbling foundation of my past. Jonathan, my wife, and almost everyone around me could see the ugly mess I was making, but I was neither able nor willing to allow wiser heads to prevail.

I felt betrayed by the church. In a fit of youthful enthusiasm while still a teenager I had pledged my life to God—lock, stock, and barrel. When my peers, the sixties generation, were "having a good time" or marching to make the world a better place, I was sweating my way through seminary. For years I had toiled in one parish after another, working impossibly long hours and thinking I was doing the will of the One whom I claimed to obey.

Yet here I was now, at that time in life when youthful idealism is inevitably tempered by the hastening approach of middle age, and I found myself asking what I had to show for the years of apparent selflessness to which I had committed myself. The only answer I could come up with was "Nothing."

Besides, what satisfaction was I getting from playing the cat-and-mouse games in which many congregations like to embroil their pastor? Always the complaints came rolling in, and it seemed that more people were dissatisfied than content with my role in parish life. Usually the gripes were not enormous, but as their numbers accumulated, the burden increased:

"Rector, I don't like the way you consecrate the elements in the Eucharist."

"Rector, that movie questioning a strong defense policy should not have been shown in our church. The president is a fine Christian man, and if he thinks that we need nuclear weapons to protect ourselves from the Russians, I back him. God isn't a pinko like you, you know."

"Rector, why are you so timid when it comes to dealing with the peace issue? I thought you were a man of principle when you arrived here, but obviously you're a closet 'conservative' like all the rest of them."

"Rector, you really aren't firm enough. Children should be seen and not heard in church. At St. Mary's they are always crying, talking, or making a nuisance of themselves. When *our* kids were little they did not behave as badly as the small fry in this congregation. You aren't firm enough with them, you know. What are you going to do about it?" And then as the final, cruel, parting shot: "Besides, the example set by your children is hardly what we would expect."

"Please excuse me, Rector, but I do think it's about time you had a haircut. . . . Oh, and by the way, tell your wife that her skirt is beautiful, but the color clashes with the blouse she's wearing."

Comments like the latter literally made me see red. Off I would clump to my office, muttering oaths to prevent myself from making a scene. Sitting there shaking with rage, I would hear a voice filtering in from the hallway. "What's gotten into Jeremy today? He seems even more bad tempered than usual."

A moment later I would hear a couple of older church members discussing the portrait of my predecessor that hangs with portraits of all the former rectors beside my office door. One would say to the other, "I do miss him, you know. He was such a godly man, and when my Jack was in the hospital that last time, he used to come and see him every day. The church isn't what it was in Father Michael's day."

On a summer morning following a series of remarks not unlike those recorded above, I stared at my increasingly haggard face in the mirror on the door of the closet in which I kept my robes. The thick hair of which I had always been so proud was thinning at the temples, here and there telltale flecks of white were appearing, and ugly crow's-feet wrinkled the skin around my eyes. Wistfully I concluded that I had ceased to be a promising young man. I had become what I was going to be. I was part of the establishment. Middle age was reaching out to grab me.

At that moment of sudden realization I was overcome by a sense of nausea and panic. "Over half my life is over: my death is nearer than my birth, and there is still so much to do and see. Damn it, I want to be young again. There are so many choices I would have made differently."

Pensively, I walked home. Since ordination, like all clergy, I had been subject to criticism and had responded by developing a thicker skin. But harsh words still hurt, especially when one's integrity was scorned as insensitive or unspiritual. Here I was pouring myself into a congregation that seemed to be composed of either smug pew warmers who thought they had all the answers or apathetic, disinterested, fair-weather parishioners.

I was indignant. "What right did they have to poke about in the privacy of my life and that of my family? Why can't they leave me alone? Why don't the troublemakers move to another church?" This latter question was an idle dream; I knew it would never happen.

I was full of bitter questions and was wondering whether it was possible to trust the God who had gotten me into this mess. When I was interviewed by St. Mary's, the church had seemed so promising. I was excited when they called me, and I dreamed about how it was going to be to become significant in the spiritual renewal of New England. On arriving, my castles in the sky collapsed, and I discovered a barrel-load of problems presided over by men and women whose lack of vision had made them prematurely old.

Out loud I exclaimed, "Damn it! Do these people know what I put myself through to minister to them? All they can do is bitch about the length of my hair or the color of my wife's blouse. It was a bad choice on her part, but I can't stand over the woman as she picks what she is to wear from her wardrobe. Why is she so incapable of developing any clothes sense?"

As I neared the front door of the house I stopped. In a blinding flash of "inspiration" I identified the snake that had coiled itself round my innards. I was forty, forty-one in a few weeks, and had achieved all I had been aiming at when I graduated from seminary.

Aloud I asked, "Where do I go from here?"

I had worked sixty- and seventy-hour weeks and had fulfilled ambitions that I thought would take a lifetime on that glorious Spring day when I had been ordained and let loose on an unsuspecting church. Now those ducks were all lined up, and I had no idea what I should aim at. That I should have set my sights so low is probably a clue to my low sense of self-esteem when I graduated from seminary. I had cloaked this problem with pious words and thoughts about humility.

Pride in my achievement was clouded by a sickening sense of dis-ease. As a young priest I had fantasized about the day when I would "arrive." I had envisioned myself being respected by my peers, co-opted onto all sorts of committees, and serving as the pastor of a large congregation. That day had come, but now it left a sour taste in my mouth.

Had it been worth it? As each week passed, my wife was becoming more of a stranger to me. And I would have been quite happy if the ground had opened up and swallowed the people among whom I ministered like the unfortunate fellow in the Old Testament whose name I can't recall.

In the months that followed, I brooded over my dilemma. How could I restore joy to my ministry? And if it were to be restored, did I even want it? Every now and again profiles of prestigious parishes would arrive, and I would be invited to apply for the job of rector. Initially I was attracted by the possibility of moving on, but as I studied these seductive documents I found myself wondering whether I had the stamina or desire to spend the rest of my life at the beck and call of a parish.

I could imagine nothing worse than pandering to the whims and fancies of the wealthy, the chic, and the divine. Anyhow, wouldn't I be exchanging one set of problems for a similar assortment in a different setting where new friendships had to be made and a fresh support system gathered?

Every now and then I would allow my name to go forward to these prosperous citadels of the Episcopal tradition. Sometime later a polite "Dear John" would come in the mail. My response would be one of both relief and anger: relief that I would not have to put myself and my family through the grueling series of interviews conducted by a group of people who were usually unclear about what they wanted in a pastor, but anger that they had raised my hopes and then dropped me. Surely they could see my abilities as a priest?

Because Dear John letters are usually sugar-coated rejections, they never actually tell the recipient why he was passed over. My old self-esteem problem would rear its ugly head, and I would read, "You're not good enough."

Thus, I found myself asking fundamental questions. When I was ordained I had thought I would work as a parish pastor for the remainder of my career. I had looked forward with anticipation to forty years of faithful service. I had idealistic visions of what it meant to be the humble servant of the servants of God. But now, a decade and a half later, the flip side of servanthood gave me a sinking feeling in the pit of my stomach. With what I thought were my best years behind me,

I could not imagine spending a quarter century doing something that had already squeezed the life from me.

"Does any man in his right mind," I thought, "voluntarily commit himself to twenty-five more years of vestry meetings? If there are 11 per year, that would mean I can look forward to sitting through 275 more. That is half as many as I have endured already, and they have taken me to the verge of madness! Then I am asked to mediate parish feuds and to show love for those whose primary goal in life seems to be to apply exquisite modes of torture to me.

*　　*　　*

On the day I first went to see Jonathan and started the counseling process, the initial problem I presented was vocational. I can remember feeling guilty as I heard myself say, "Jonathan, I can't stand my job. I'm not boasting when I say I know I'm good at it. Everyone tells me St. Mary's is a difficult congregation and that I have done a sterling job of turning lead into gold, but I can't see myself keeping at it for much longer."

He started exploring the points of stress with which I wrestled.

"What upsets you about it?"

"Everything."

"Be more specific."

"That's hard, but I suppose I am sick to death of people laying all of their trips on me. I am fed up with never being able to escape from the job. I have precious little time to myself, and for all the work I do, I am miserably underpaid. I resent never having weekends. When I take my life in my hands and am totally honest about my struggles, I am made to feel guilty because it has been suggested that a priest should not have those sort of difficulties. Frankly, I am expected to play a particular role for which I am patently unsuited."

"Few clergy are capable of handling the role expectations their congregations lay on them," Jonathan interjected. I never heard him, for I had already darted off in another direction.

"*They* can have their highs and lows, and *they* can come in the middle of the winter and pour their depression and frustration over me, but *I'm* not allowed to experience troughs and valleys. If I ever tell anyone that I go through similar periods of disintegration, eyebrows are raised, and I'm made to feel that a priest should not be human."

By the end of this tirade I could feel the anger rising within me. I was articulating notions that had been buried deep within me. Beads of sweat formed on my forehead, and a knot tightened in my stomach. For months all I had wanted to tell my parishioners was, "Just leave me alone. Let me crawl into a hole and wallow in my own misery. Allow me to sleep. Give me a break. Let me have a year's sabbatical to help me get my act together again."

In my imagination I heard these words spilling out of a particularly pugnacious little man who had the uncanny gift of rubbing me the wrong way: "A sabbatical? Ho, ho, ho! You work only a day a week as it is. I've worked for the phone company for nearly thirty years, and they never gave me a sabbatical, so why should we give you one?"

Yet I knew that if I could take a year's sabbatical, I would never return to St. Mary's. The people would then have made an investment from which they would not benefit. My conscience prevented me from following this course of action. It would be wrong to rip them off in this way.

For several weeks the counselor and I had talked around the issue of my vocational discontent. Clearly it had its roots in my allowing myself to be overworked—to overachieve and not know when to give myself the time needed to restore my equilibrium. But there was more to my malaise than the problem I presented.

Not only was I asking some of those fundamental questions that torment all men as they enter midlife, but I was also struggling with a drivenness that had characterized my life since childhood. Matters were made worse by the fact that I had achieved so much so quickly that now I did not know how to follow my own act in succeeding years and wasn't sure that I really wanted to.

As I have said already, on graduating from seminary I had set myself what I thought were tough career objectives. The initial years of my ministry suggested that my estimation of myself was right, and I would have a hard job fulfilling those ambitions. However, as time passed my self-confidence grew, and a variety of opportunities began opening up. And if they didn't come naturally, I discovered ways to encourage them along. Now I had reached an impasse: what I had thought were realistic goals for a lifetime I had achieved by my thirty-ninth birthday.

The only "honor" that had not come my way was election as a bishop, and I was not sure this was something I wanted. I had watched episcopal elections take place and was not prepared to put myself through that process. Anyhow, there were certain "bishopy" attributes that I knew were missing from my make-up. Maybe the realization of this made me listless.

So what was I to do with the rest of my life? In one guise or another, this was the question with which I bombarded the long-suffering Jonathan. Here I was—at a point where I could still make a significant midcourse correction and get away with it. A few years down the line that would be impossible. If I let the opportunity escape, I was doomed to spend the rest of my life on the treadmill of parish ministry. When I first went to see Jonathan I could only fume about the miseries of ministry, for the way ahead seemed totally unclear.

Later we would be able to look back on the procession of events and see how order had been restored after a period of monumental disarray. I was no longer a parish priest, it was true, but I was now in an area of ministry that was more to my liking after a spell in the doldrums.

But to get from there to here I had to enter a cold, black tunnel, experience the "dark night of the soul," or whatever you want to call it. I felt myself pondering a frigid and empty vacuum into which I would surely tumble and disappear forever.

In retrospect I am able to see that my love for pastoral ministry had been waning for a long time. Slowly, people pressures had sucked the life from me. Instead of reading the signs of the situation correctly and giving myself more space, I had turned up the heat. Had I been more sensible, perhaps I would still be finding satisfaction as a parish priest, although probably not at St. Mary's.

On that last afternoon in Jonathan's office I looked across at him and smilingly said, "It was ridiculous, wasn't it?"

He nodded and then was silent for a long time mulling over the follow-up question that I put to him, "Why did I throw myself so unreservedly into everything rather than pulling back and treating myself with the care that I so obviously required?"

At last he spoke. "You were frightened. You couldn't make out what was happening. You dealt with the problem the only way you knew how—you worked. For a long time work has been your primary source of gratification, so you turned to your job, hoping that it would give you the strokes it had provided in the past. This time, instead of helping you over the ditch, it dug a deeper one."

"I suppose this is true of clergy as a whole," I replied. "By and large, we tend to be workaholics incapable of knowing when to let up. I was no exception. On top of that, when I work I am obsessive, and that stubbornness that had always enabled me to follow through and complete a task had, on this occasion, propelled me down an increasingly slippery slope."

My friend nodded. "Have you got that obsession under control?"

I laughed, "Does an obsessive ever get it under control?"

I thought for a moment, then continued, "At present it would be fair to say that I am better equipped to diagnose the symptoms and can head off the worst consequences, but who's to say that I won't fall into the same trap in the future?

I will be a lot more careful, but I'm not sure I'm totally able to help myself."

A long silence followed as we stared at each other, Jonathan eager to get something else out of me. I had nothing to say, so I let him sit there puffing his pipe. At last he spoke, and in my mind I chalked up a small victory in the "game of silence."

"When eventually we get together again, there is an interesting vein of gold to be mined in there somewhere."

I smiled, recognizing the glint in my friend's eye. Although I thought we had reached the bottom of the complexities of my personality, in his perception there were many other facets of Jeremy Wilkinson that might upset the boat again and leave me thrashing around in deep water. After pondering his words for a moment, I changed the subject.

4

Ironically, when I first went to see Jonathan, the passport for escape from St. Mary's was sitting on the coffee table at home. I was being vigorously courted by an affluent parish in a delightful part of Maryland. They had heard about me, and it seemed I was at the top of their list of prospective rectors. It was the sort of job opportunity that clergy spend their lives dreaming about but seldom get.

The congregational profile that had been sent was impressive, as was the salary they were prepared to pay. But the more I examined the possibility, the less attractive it seemed. The thought of getting caught in the vortex of another parish's life frightened me: the petty politics, the nit-picking that goes on at vestry meetings, the endless round of calling on the sick and elderly, the pouring out of myself on behalf of others, and so on and so on.

I tried to look the possibility in the eye, and as I did I knew there was no way I could consider making such a move at this time in my life. Were I to get the job, I would probably be a liability from the word "go." Anyhow, I knew I could not hold out emotionally until they were ready to make their call. Every fiber of my being wanted to move on, yet I was now convinced that I had unfinished business with myself that had to be completed in this setting before I could depart.

Never in my life have I so yearned to escape from somewhere. I felt psychologically battered and bruised, and the resentment I harbored toward those I served had been degenerating into a spiteful kind of hatred during the past few

37

months. For all my faults, this was something new to me, and I found myself struggling to come to grips with loathesome and alien emotions.

I was bitter. Whatever I did, they took me for granted. I worked myself into the ground on their behalf, but instead of receiving thanks or commendation, I became the recipient of an endless string of snide comments. No doubt my apparently easygoing manner and sense of humor led parishioners to believe I could be the butt of an endless string of jokes, but the years had now worn me out.

It hurt dreadfully to be told, even if in jest, "I wish I could work only one day a week, like you" or "I'd love to sit at home all day studying the Bible and reading books, but I have a family to support."

Couldn't the idiots who said these things see that I sometimes worked as many as eighty hours per week, often undertaking ministries that they were either too lazy or too preoccupied to engage in? In addition, each summer when they scooted off to their cottages in the mountains of New Hampshire, or on the coast of Maine, or on Martha's Vineyard, it was my job to keep the church going.

"How lovely it must be to leave the office at five on a Friday evening and not have to think about it again until Monday morning," I would muse as I walked my dog or tried to sandwich time with my children in between the demands of parishioners, an endless round of meetings, and increasing church responsibilities.

I cannot describe the sense of utter hopelessness that swept over me most mornings when I arrived at the church, unlocked my office door, and got going with the day's work. One morning I received an enthusiastic call from a colleague in South Carolina who, after we had completed the business that had prompted the call, bubbled over with high spirits as he told me how well things were going.

I could not bring myself to tell him how miserable I was feeling, so when he asked me I just made light of it and said, "A bit weary, but I'm okay," and changed the subject. In my mind his name was dropped from the list of people I wanted to talk to again, and as time passed, that list had been shrinking perilously. Only recently have I started to make contact with some of them again.

At the outset of my ministry in that part of Boston I had thought the parish was made up of a homogeneous bunch of straightforward, undemanding, suburban people. What a relief that would be after the multitude of prima donnas in my last place. How wrong initial impressions can be! As I started peeling off the layers and getting under its skin, I found myself engulfed in an incredibly complex set of problems.

Most parishes are far less easy to read than they initially appear, but this one took the gold medal as far as I was concerned. In the end I decided the candidates who came for the interview needed lots of luck or the perception of Sherlock Holmes if they were to uncover the problems at St. Mary's.

I had been in the parish only a short time before I was forced to admit that this was not a good fit for either the congregation or for our family. Not only was St. Mary's a more difficult parish than I have space to describe, but as I looked at myself, it was obvious that I possessed the wrong set of skills and interests to lead them far on the next stage of their spiritual journey.

Had I been a little less stubborn, I would probably have stayed long enough to make myself thoroughly unpopular by breaking a few of the logjams that impeded progress in parish life. Then I would have sought a new job. I would soon have been rewriting my resume and looking for a setting that suited us far better. Alas, I did not. So by the time I took my problems to Jonathan, my psychological health had reached a dangerously low ebb.

Determined to succeed where everyone told me I was bound to fail, I dug in for a long siege. When I arrived and began getting to know the bishop and my fellow clergy, a surprisingly accurate picture of the parish's past was painted for me. Heads would shake, and I knew their prognosis of my future was not good. Undeterred, I soldiered on. In my mind's eye I regarded myself as a knight in shining armor courageously riding out to tackle the dragons that lurked in the nether reaches and dark places of the congregation.

During my first years of working as a youth minister in a large suburban parish, my boss had accused me of having a "Messiah complex." I had vigorously denied his analysis, but now as an older and wiser man, I am forced to concede that he was nearer the mark than I was prepared to acknowledge at that time. This was something Jonathan and I spent hours working on. I suppose there are a surprisingly large number of clergy rather like me. I had been crusading to put St. Mary's right; unfortunately, I was unprepared to admit I had bitten off more than I could chew.

However, it would be churlish to blame my burnout solely on that particular congregation. A parish's personality takes several generations to create; its present members are the most recent recipients of an established tradition. The five years I spent there was an unfortunate confluence of that church's long-established neurosis and mine.

We wrestled with each other. To this modest little community of faith I brought my own tattered patchwork of triumphs and disasters. I was no saint, and my own soul bore the scars and wrinkles of my life's journey. While my ministry there was to have some positive effect, the interplay of my quirks with their accumulated history was to so damage me that an extended period of therapy would be the only way that I would rediscover myself and find healing.

Despite the negative comments I have made about St. Mary's, my years there were not without highlights. We wept together, and we rejoiced together. Even while I was floundering in the depths of despair there were moments and occasions that I will treasure for the remainder of my years on earth.

You cannot pray at a sickbed or comfort a grieving widow without creating invisible bonds with a parish family that can never be completely severed. I defy any pastor to cradle an infant in his arms, baptizing him or her in the name of the Father, Son, and Holy Spirit, and marking his or her forehead with the sign of the cross, and not develop an affinity with the parents and community in which the little one will grow up.

The best illustration I can find to describe St. Mary's is as an aging beauty, frantically scrambling to hide the blemishes and crow's-feet that advancing years bring under an ever-thicker layer of cosmetics. The parish had a fine past, but that attractive church set in a quiet corner of a leafy suburb now gave a false impression of emotional and spiritual health. Instead of being willing to face up to the unpleasant business of dealing with the ravages of time, the congregation had unconsciously conspired to deny the changes wrought by the years, covering them with make-up and saccharine sweetness.

I had been a priest long enough to know I would begin to discover a complex network of relationships as I delved beneath the superficialities presented to me when I began as rector of St. Mary's. I had a shrewd idea that I was in for a rough ride, but then I am not sure any congregation can be described as "easy." However, I was not prepared for the tangled web of neuroses and unresolved conflicts that I found.

*   *   *

The parish is not the subject of this book; it plays a major role, amplifying my own difficulties, but as we explore what made me burn out, most of the clues can be found inside me. Suffice it to say that a steady diet of mixed signals and extraordinary hidden agendas did not make for good mental health.

It was like an ill-advised marriage. Hardly had it begun than I wanted our relationship to end, as if the parish were a girl whom I was merely dating. But we had moved into their house: the knot had been well and truly tied. So I committed myself to saving the church from itself. Even if the chance to leave had presented itself early in my career at St. Mary's, I'm not sure I would have taken it.

But no matter how we tried, the fabric of my past and theirs would not meld. To continue the marriage analogy, we were never able to reach a high enough level of trust to be

41

able to confront our differences and work them through from a standpoint of mutual respect. There was always an undertow, even when the surface seemed as calm as a millpond.

As with most new pastorates, we experienced a brief honeymoon period. But with twenty-twenty hindsight I can see the storm clouds looming on the horizon even then. With the exception of a handful, I rapidly reached the conclusion that I did not even like the congregation. Their tastes were at variance with mine, their spirituality was at odds with my own, and there were times when I wondered whether we even worshiped the same God!

Certainly, the parish had been influenced by a style of Christianity that clashed with the expressions of that faith that were at the heart of my spiritual journey. Initially, I thought that I would be enriched and that we could meld our differences into a richer whole, but such an exercise requires give and take. It soon became clear that these diversities would never be compatible.

I have always loved my Anglican heritage, but many of the opinion-formers at St. Mary's had a rather jaundiced opinion of the church to which they belonged. We certainly had more than our fair share of problems at the time, but these people would have been quite happy if we had made a unilateral declaration of independence and gone our own separate ways. That I am still a loyal member of the church of my birth today is evidence of my commitment to its principles.

During my first month on board we held an overnight planning session at someone's cottage in the White Mountains. I had looked forward to this as an occasion to get to know the leadership of the congregation, share our dreams, and find ways to forge a working partnership. I came away downhearted because it was clear that the direction they wanted to go was not one in which I was able to take them.

Of course there is a flip side of this conundrum: I was not prepared to let them set an agenda that would trap me with a program and style with which I was at odds. I was willing to

42

compromise on things, but it was against my nature to roll over and play dead.

The stage was set. Seeds of discord had been sown in fertile soil. They would germinate in the ensuing years and relentlessly encroach on every area of our life. Those whose antennae were well tuned or who were looking for an excuse to jump ship soon disappeared. During that first year the congregation visibly shrank, and my detractors blamed me.

Unbeknown to me, several families had decided before I even arrived that unless I turned out to be the archangel Gabriel, they would leave the parish. But as the procession out of the back door of the church got underway, the self-doubt that had plagued me in earlier years came to the fore again. The experience was sickening and frustrating. I had been mortally wounded without knowing it, and the downhill slide had begun.

A handful of the evacuees from St. Mary's had the courage to tell me they were going, and I respect them for it. There were several cold, snowy afternoons during that first winter when people sat in my office and explained to me that "the Lord had called them" to join another congregation. On the surface these interviews were all sweetness and light, but underneath I felt I was being kicked hard in the solar plexus without being given the opportunity to defend myself or fight back.

Others who departed would not talk about it but would write a letter informing me of their intentions. Some just disappeared. Sometimes I discovered their exodus after they had already joined another church. Some of those who stayed resented me for "chasing away" their friends. Yet as newcomers appeared, these people tended to be highly selective of those they welcomed. Those note considered potential allies were not made to feel at home. Often these were the sort of folk that I would have loved to have gathered around me, but before long they were off visiting other congregations and a majority of them soon disappeared.

My early months at St. Mary's were made uncomfortable by the knowledge that a group had begun to form after I had been there a matter of weeks to see whether they could oust me. Not many weeks before, some of the ringleaders had elected me their rector, but already they had lost confidence in me. The rationale for their actions was all wrapped up in pious language; the reality was that they discovered, to their horror, that I would not endorse everything they wanted for the parish.

I am no stranger to congregational conflict, but until I came to St. Mary's, difficulties with colleagues and parishioners had usually been temporary. I have my jagged edges, but I am not *that* difficult to get along with. Every setting in which I have ministered has had its awkward squad, and I have made more than my fair share of silly mistakes. Previously I had been able to sit down with those with whom I was at odds, and we managed to hammer out our difficulties. Only now am I beginning to see why that was impossible at St. Mary's.

Soon after I became a minister my path was crossed by a particularly difficult woman who "got at" me no matter what I did. Eventually, to our mutual surprise, we found ourselves on the same side in a conflict. That resulted in a relationship that enabled us to resolve our differences. But at St. Mary's I cannot remember anything like that happening. Getting conflicts out into the open and dealing with them in a healthy manner seemed beyond the resources of a majority of this congregation.

Whenever unpleasantness flared up, it was unacknowledged or pushed beneath the surface accompanied by appropriate religious language. Like a forceful stream in a limestone valley, it would go underground, gathering momentum all the time. The people at St. Mary's had been handling unpleasantness in this pattern for so long that I was powerless to bring more than a handful of problems to the surface, only then to be disarmed.

The bane of St. Mary's was "unspoken conflict." Not until my final months there had we made enough progress for troublesome issues to be aired. By then it was too late for me, and no sooner was I gone than the lid was firmly pressed back on again. Having lived in the midst of this conundrum for so long and having set myself up as the conduit through which destructive, high voltage currents had to pass, my circuits were overloaded, my fuses were ready to blow.

The prestigious parish in Baltimore whose profile sat fat and inviting on the coffee table beckoned seductively. Yet each time I examined the document I was further repelled by the prospect. I should have been flattered that they were interested in having me as their rector, but at that moment I saw it as just another arena in which I would get eaten alive by a pride of Christians fashionably dressed in lions' clothing.

Imperceptibly I began to despise Christians for the way I had allowed them to treat me. I started hating the church in general and this parish in particular. To make matters worse, I hated myself for nurturing such feelings. A tangled knot of hostile feelings had wrapped around my inmost being, and I was at a loss to know how I might untie it.

I expressed my disgust with an irrational hatred of God, whom I felt had betrayed me. Surely he could see the mess he had gotten me into. I felt myself sinking. The further I was sucked into the mire, the more I screamed for help. When no answer seemed to come, I reached the hasty conclusion that the Almighty was no longer interested in me.

In anguish my wonderings about the Deity I had pledged to serve started to take a sinister turn. My hatred turned to doubt, and the next logical step was to deny that he ever existed. If that were the case, then why should I bother to worship and serve him? Beneath me loomed the abyss. Could I discard God as an unnecessary figment of the collective human imagination?

With all my heart I longed to break the habit of this divinity and be freed from my bondage to him. Did I have the nerve to take that step? Could I handle the accompanying guilt? What would happen to me?

5

My demeanor during that wrap-up session with Jonathan was very different from my first experience of therapy. On that first visit I had been paralyzed by fear of what was happening to me. This was intensified by my recognition that he would find out things about me that I had never shared even with my nearest and dearest. My misgivings were not without foundation, but as a result of all that had happened, I felt more at home with myself than ever before.

At that last meeting, in the midst of the serious business, we played verbal games with one another. While the counselor does learn his client's most intimate secrets, the relationship is not a one-way street. This man and I had become fast friends as a result of the hundreds of hours we had spent together. Our companionship on that final afternoon reflected it.

Each of us had experienced growth. Jonathan was even better equipped to handle other pastors who got themselves into similar trouble; I was more poised, self-confident, and at home with myself. Each morning as I examined the image in the shaving mirror, I had no option but to admit that I looked disgustingly healthy, a far cry from the wraith who had dragged himself into the counseling center for that first session.

But my return to psychological and physical health had come with a large price tag. The whole process had forced me to reach inward and, to my surprise, discover resources that I had not known were there. For me, a private sort of person, therapy was like squeezing blood from the proverbial stone and discovering that there actually was some there.

During those months Jonathan and I often talked of death and resurrection: it was one of the recurring themes of our encounters. Life is a process of little deaths followed by risings from the tomb of the past. As we sat and enjoyed each other's company during that last counseling hour, this topic was raised again. We both agreed that I had come through a substantial experience of "death" and that a glorious resurrection had taken place.

"You know," I mused, "this crisis I've come through has brought an unexpected quality to my faith that was not there before."

"What do you mean?" came the question.

"Well, while there are only minimal changes in the substance of my belief, I am finding facets opening themselves to me as never before. There are subtleties to which I was once blind that I now can see."

He nodded, encouraging me to carry on. I paused, then spoke again. "Perhaps there are resurrection eyes with which you see that much more clearly after an experience like mine. I have a better grasp of myself and of who I am, and as a result I have a new appreciation of the grace and loving-kindness of God. Until all this happened, my preaching had a harsh and unyielding edge. But I think I've softened it now. I've discovered the gentleness of the Holy God."

Jonathan nodded again, and once more the room was silent.

In my mind I played back what I had said. Yes, the rising again had ushered in a new life different from all that had gone before, and yet I was still the same. In the healing process I had not sacrificed my identity; I had found it. I had been able to discard baggage from the past that was not conducive to growth. Like a phoenix, a more mature and less fraught individual had risen from the ashes. I had returned to the business of living, and I was better equipped to avoid some of my previously self-destructive patterns.

I had started down that slippery slope by ignoring clouds of depression that, no matter what, would not go away. Winston Churchill once described depression as a "black dog"; while being chased over hill and dale by a plague of dogs, I had with determination ignored my inmost self and put out a sign saying, "Business as usual." And business as usual involved attempting to flush out my troubles by living life more frenetically.

Like others who have been sucked into the vortex, the event that precipitated the sickening downward spiral was relatively insignificant: I had trouble with my car.

*   *   *

I was returning from visiting an elderly pillar of the congregation who had gone to live with his daughter in a pleasant little town forty minutes or so south of Boston. Negotiating my way through rush-hour traffic, my car decided it had had enough and sputtered to a halt.

Massachusetts drivers leave something to be desired in the best of times, but on this occasion I seemed to be caught in the lemming-like rush of hundreds of men and women for whom it had been a bad day at the office. My misfortune made me the butt of ill-tempered jeers and insults as the blockage slowed the traffic down to a walking pace.

Feeling like a fool and with the help of an unusually surly traffic cop, I arranged for the AAA to send out a tow truck from a nearby garage to remove the offending vehicle from blocking the lunatic flight from the city. There were no mechanics on duty, so I had to wait until the next day to find out what was wrong. Actually, it took the on-site expert less than half an hour to identify the trouble and put it right. How I wished I knew more about the mysteries of the internal combustion engine!

From a grease-covered phone that nuzzled up against an equally oily Coke machine, I managed to reach Henry Chew, one of that handful of people in my congregation whom I considered a personal friend. He came out, picked me up, and dropped me off at home.

As humiliating as these experiences are, most of us are able to take them in our stride. They are little hiccups in the flow of life. We are embarrassed and upset when they happen, but once they are over we can usually see the funny side of the catastrophe and turn it into a conversation piece to amuse friends over the dinner table. Although I may get bad-tempered, such situations do not normally throw me, but this was the last straw. The camel's back could take no more; it broke, and my descent into hell began.

Worse still was the sense of forlornness I experienced sitting in an empty house. My family was on vacation with relatives for a couple of weeks, and I felt very lonely. I wanted someone to hug me, mother me, tell me that it was all right, but no one was there. A drinker would have turned to booze. I was tempted to open a fresh bottle of wine and drink myself into oblivion. Finally I settled on the strong cup of tea that my English grandmother always prescribed on such occasions.

Half an hour later, as I sat sipping my third cup, utterly paralyzed and unable to think of what to do next, the doorbell rang. There, standing on the doorstep, was Rebecca Chew, Henry's wife. She had grabbed a meal from her freezer, defrosted it in the microwave, and brought it to me.

I thanked her profusely and hoped she would go away so that I could throw the food into the trash can and continue to wallow in my misery. But Rebecca was not a woman who could be put off lightly. She brushed past me and marched into the kitchen. Soon the table was set and what I would normally have regarded as an appetizing dish was placed in front of me. Then she insisted on staying to watch me eat because, as she put it, "It will do you a world of good, Jeremy."

"But, Becca, I'm not hungry. I'm not sure I will ever be able to eat anything again," I responded, exaggerating for effect.

"Nonsense! Now sit down and let me get everything ready."

My protests were in vain, but it was pleasant to have some

company. I pulled up my chair and tried to make small talk. Considering the situation in which I found myself, this was not particularly easy.

Henry and Rebecca were in the middle of the stormiest chapter of their not altogether satisfactory marriage. We had spent many hours together talking about it, but their problems were beyond my ability. When I admitted to myself and to them that we had reached an impasse, I referred them to a family therapist who was better equipped to help them with their difficulties.

Only after my problem with the car did I discover that they had seriously started talking about separation the previous weekend. Why they never got anywhere with the counselor mystified me. They normally were not people who refused a challenge, but when it came to their own relationship they seemed unwilling to stick with it. I should have realized there was a third party, but for some reason the fact escaped me.

Henry managed to get a transfer to his firm's Los Angeles office and took his secretary with him. Rebecca presented herself as the wronged wife to the watching world, and everyone sympathized. Many months later I heard the other side from Henry who was back in town on business. Piecing both of their stories together, neither of them came out smelling particularly sweet.

But I am rushing ahead of myself.

With this eager, attractive woman looking on, I managed to stuff most of her beef stroganoff down my throat, although it must have taken a pot of coffee and several glasses of water to wash it down. I'm sure it was delicious, but as far as my churning insides were concerned, I might have been devouring human flesh. This was about the last decent meal I ate for months. My sharpest memory was of violent indigestion all night and countless trips to the bathroom!

The meal over, I saw my guest to the door. "However can I thank you for coming to the aid of a weary traveler in distress," I said with forced lightheartedness. I was generous in my expressions of gratitude for her thoughtfulness, but I missed the note of warning injected into her final comment.

"Don't even bother to worry about it, Jerry, dear," came the immediate response. She smiled wistfully and went on, "What you need now is to have a shower and go to bed with an Agatha Christie and gentle music in the background."

"Well, thank Henry for allowing me the pleasure of your food and your company for an hour."

Here was the part of the exchange that my normally well-attuned ear should have picked up: "Oh, Henry had nothing to do with it. I was *very* concerned about you. *He* suddenly got a call from his secretary. The boss wanted him back at the office to deal with some emergency that has arisen on the West Coast. He went running off to worship at the shrine of his work—his one true love—and I was left by myself. I *do* hate being by myself, so as we were both going to be alone, and you were obviously in need, I decided to do something about it. Now kiss me goodnight, open the door, and I'll drop by tomorrow to see how you're doing. It would never do for Rachel to come home and find you a bag of bones."

As she stood there in the dim light she looked extraordinarily appealing. Her perfume hung enticingly on the humidity of the warm night air. Her eyes sparkled, and her mouth turned upwards in a little grin that expressed concern and yet at the same time taunted me.

Without thinking, I leaned over with the intention of brushing her cheek in the accepted style of social kiss, but her lips got in the way, and the resulting kiss was returned with passionate tenderness. I instinctively pulled back while still savoring the sweetness of the forbidden moment.

She patted me on the cheek and whispered, "You're a wonderful man, Jeremy Wilkinson, and don't you forget it."

Then she was gone. As I watched the taillights of her car disappear down the road, I was in an even greater state of panic and shock. Having closed the door, I felt myself being squeezed from every side by uncontrollable pangs of guilt.

I slept increasingly badly that night and the nights that followed. I would wake in the morning drenched in sweat and feeling nauseous. My dreams were jangled nightmares where whatever happened seemed to take place to the accompaniment of blaring horns in the middle of the crowded highway coming from Boston. Something inside me had snapped: I knew I must do something about it, but just what I was not sure. During the days that followed, far from subsiding, the storm got worse.

The next Sunday as I presided at the celebration of the Holy Eucharist the words almost stuck in my throat. I wondered whether the congregation made any sense of the sermon that I preached. If they did, then they were more intelligent than I. It came out like so much gobbledegook. I went home and threw up. Feeling utterly exhausted, I washed my blotchy face and resolved to chat with a Methodist minister-friend, older and wiser than I. I had to bare my soul to him and ask for guidance.

*   *   *

Brian's favorite eating place was an old-fashioned diner in a rather down-at-the-heel section of Revere. The owner was a jolly Italian whose English was terrible but whose food was magnificent. Whenever I went there I found Alphonso's accent too thick to understand, so Brian would act as interpreter. Alphonso thought it hilarious—an American who didn't speak English well enough to converse with him. He, Alphonso, had come from a tiny village near Naples thirty years ago and was fluent.

"Whatta is a-wrong with you, Padre? I givva de best Eenglish lessons ina Boston. . . . Ha, ha, ha."

We found a quiet corner table, and while I gulped at my coffee I spilled my pain all over the white-haired saint who sat before me devouring the largest submarine sandwich I had ever seen in my life. He was a seasoned veteran who had experienced the ups and downs of ministry for thirty years. That was why I needed his counsel. This time I knew I was in too deep to dig myself out on my own.

Brian had seen many promising clergy come and go. I had heard him tell of a string of prodigies who would take on local congregations, make a tremendous hit for a while, then run out of steam. Some would lose their vision and opt for another ministry, others would settle for unchallenging mediocrity, and still others would blow up like Mount St. Helens.

"All over this country, Jeremy, there are pastors in churches of every tradition who have lost their vision. They drive themselves until they are drained of all their goodness and then hang on until retirement, whether that be five or twenty-five years away."

These were hardly heartening words, but I knew they were true. I had seen these walking wounded at clergy gatherings and had secretly prayed, "Lord, please don't let me become like that."

When I got to telling him about Rebecca and the night my car had broken down, my face burned. I mumbled something about it not being too difficult to have an affair with so attractive a woman. I told him how many times I had replayed that evening in my mind and watched her with her flowing hair and turquoise blue dress jump enthusiastically into her car and wiggle her fingers at me in a wave as she disappeared out of sight.

Brian broke into my meanderings.

"Jerry, let me give you a word of advice, for what it's worth. You are a fine priest. I have watched your ministry in a very difficult setting, and I believe you have a grand future before you. But before you can move on to the next chapter, you have some ghosts that need to be dispelled. They have probably been hanging around for years, but you can't put the exorcism off any longer. Get yourself some good counseling before it's too late and a promising future is turned into a shattered dream."

"I guess that is what I wanted you to say. My ministry seems to be in tatters, and my marriage is none too safe. I can't eat, I can't sleep, and I am starting to think I am losing my sanity."

Brian smiled gently. In that smile was all the love of Christ. I could see why his congregation adored him. He had been there for years, and although the church was not big, it had a quality that I had not seen many other places. He seemed to know the way of the world, and yet he was completely selfless at the same time—truly "an Israelite without guile."

"You're not going mad. You're troubled, yes, but crazy—never."

There was silence for a moment while an idea crystallized in my mind.

"Couldn't I spend time working this through with you?" I asked impulsively, frightened at the idea of spilling my life's secrets to some psychologist. I was not ready for that kind of invasion of my privacy. Few of us ever are.

Without losing that gentle smile, my friend looked me straight in the eye, shook his head, and said, "No. I'm just a simple pastor, Jerry. My yearning has always been to proclaim the gospel like John Wesley, stand firm upon the truth like Martin Luther, and love all God's creatures like St. Francis of Assisi. I am not able to give the help that you need. I can only be your friend and suggest the direction in which you might head. I think you are asking me to walk that road for you."

Those words undid me. My head dropped between my arms, and I sprawled across the table, weeping like a baby. Never before had I been able to cry so readily. I felt Brian's hand on my shoulder, but it was many minutes before I could recover myself enough to complete the conversation.

By the time I was feeling up to leaving Alphonso's diner, we had talked some more about whom I might see and how to get started. I had directed others to a counselor many times, but now I allowed myself to be instructed like a neophyte by my friend.

His parting words were sobering: "Be very wary of Rebecca. You aren't the first minister who has encountered an alluring woman, and you won't be the last. Remember, there are certain women who consider a minister a particular challenge."

"Oh, not Rebecca. She knows Rachel, and she wouldn't do that."

"Don't be so sure of that, my friend. God bless you."

Starting my car, I knew that I did not have a moment to

lose. I had to call Jonathan and call quickly. The longer I delayed the less likely I was to go through with it. I was terrified at what might happen. I did not want therapy because I did not want to meet the dark side of my soul. But I had asked Brian's advice knowing that I had to be willing to take it.

Arriving home, I went into my study and found Jonathan's number in the phone book. With shaking hand and sweaty palm I dialed the number. It rang several times, and I thought, "Good, there's no one there."

Just as I was about to hang up, Jonathan himself answered the phone.

"Jerry," he greeted me as I introduced myself, "sorry I took so long, but our receptionist had to take her son to the doctor, so I'm minding the store. Well, how are you? I haven't seen you for ages, not since the diocesan convention. How's life at St. Mary's, then?"

I cleared my throat, cut through the small talk, and blurted out my problem. Jonathan was silent at the end of the line, and I knew that he was waiting for more. At last I brought myself to say, "Jonathan, I need to come and see you."

"Grand. How does four o'clock today sound to you?"

"That's okay. And I know how to get there."

6

When talking with friends about these events in my life, I have flippantly said that counseling broke my fall. But when talking to myself, I have not been so certain. Recently, as I was driving on a long trip, I pondered these events. Now I think that it is likely that therapy accelerated that fall, forcing me to confront some of the many "demons" trapped deep within my psyche.

I am not saying that counseling is unhelpful in such circumstances. Although therapy may have hastened my initial decline, the relationship I was forging with Jonathan was establishing a safety net. So when I did tumble, I did not fall into the abyss. I was caught in a net that made it possible for me to build anew after the hurricane had passed.

At first counseling contributed to violent mood swings. Once I had taken the plunge I was exhilarated that I was doing something about my inner turmoil. But the lows were sickening. It happened that I was on a high when Rachel and our children returned from their trip to see their grandparents in Florida and friends in Washington, D.C., and Philadelphia.

Excitedly, like a kid with a new toy, I told Rachel what was happening. I had kept this from her when we had spoken on the phone, fearing her negative response. She had always expressed misgivings about the counseling profession. My fears were justified. She was horrified when she learned that I had put myself under the care of a psychologist. Hurt and bewildered that I had been so secretive, she used her fluent command of the English language to make it plain that, while this might be okay for me, I was to count her out.

"I don't believe in counselors or in any of the tribe of headshrinkers, and from what I have seen since getting home, I don't think Jonathan is doing you any good," she pouted. "You're a totally different person from the one I left three weeks ago. Look what that fool has done in a short time: God knows what you'll be like in three months."

Having uttered these prophetic words, she ran upstairs, locked herself in the bedroom, and wept profusely for nearly an hour. She came downstairs with red eyes and sulked as she went about her chores, refusing to talk or raise the subject again. I was too wrapped up in myself to be particularly aware of her struggle after that outburst. But that was not all: two crises were about to break upon the parish that would totally undo me.

*   *   *

The first crisis came as a phone call early one Saturday morning. As usual, I had not been able to get off to sleep for hours. But hardly more than an hour after sliding into a restless slumber, I was awakened by the jangle of Alexander Graham Bell's confounded invention and a series of sharp digs in the ribs from my wife urging me to answer it before it woke the children.

I was in a dazed state, and it must have taken me a good sixty seconds before I managed to decipher the sobs at the other end of the line. I recognized the distraught voice of Caroline Cunningham at the end of the line, one of the sweetest and most generous people in my congregation.

"Oh, Jeremy . . . I . . . I. . . . Please come quickly. . . . I . . . I . . . need your . . . help. . . ." Her words trailed away, and in sleepy confusion I tried to get her to explain to me what was troubling her. I was not ready for her answer.

"I'm . . . I'm . . . at . . . at . . . Massachusetts General. . . . I'm afraid I'm going to lose Lewis. . . ." She completely came apart at that point, and I could make no further sense of her words. By now I was wide awake, as was Rachel.

Fortunately, Caroline had a nurse at her side, who, in a calm, collected, and professional manner, told me that Lewis Cunningham had been brought straight to Emergency from a concert at Symphony Hall, where he had passed out. He was comatose on arrival and had never recovered consciousness. He was in Intensive Care, but his vital signs were ebbing fast, and they did not think that he could last much longer. Caroline wanted me there when it happened.

"But, Nurse, you haven't told me what happened."

"We're pretty certain he has a massive cerebral hemorrhage. The tests we have been able to do suggest little can be done other than to keep him comfortable."

"Thank you," I mumbled in shock and panic. Automatically I got up, showered, and dressed while trying to explain to Rachel what seemed to have happened. She immediately broke into tears, and that was more than I could handle. I was having enough trouble coping with myself; I could not cope with her as well. I fled downstairs. Every window in the house must have rattled as I slammed the door with all the anger I could muster.

Traffic was light at that hour. The sun was just rising, and it promised to be a perfect day. After stopping to buy a large cup of coffee, I maneuvered my car into the fast lane and took off at high speed, thankful that on Saturdays commuters were few in number.

Unfortunately, I failed to account for the police. As I opened her up, experiencing that heady sensation of speed so seldom possible on an urban highway, I became a moving target for any weary cop along my route. Barely two miles down the road, before I had had a sip from the steaming coffee cup perched precariously on the dash, I felt my heart sink. In the mirror I saw blue flashing lights closing in on me.

Pulling onto the hard shoulder, I sat cursing as he drew in behind me and cautiously approached the driver's window.

"Well now, this isn't a raceway, you know. You came past

me at eighty-one miles an hour and haven't slowed down much since. . . ."

Then he caught sight of the clerical collar. "Father, you should know better than that. . . . Coming home from a party are you?"

"Just my luck," I thought. "I've got the joker of the highway patrol."

"No, Officer, and neither am I looking for an illustration for tomorrow morning's sermon. Actually, I'm rushing to get to the bedside of a man who's fearfully ill at Mass General. If possible, I want to be there before he dies."

The ticket never got written. The cop's face lit up, and he sprinted to his cruiser yelling, "Follow me. I'll escort you there. Nothing like a good emergency to get the juices flowing!"

I wish that he hadn't been so eager to help, because by the time I reached the hospital, two more cruisers had joined us, sirens wailing. I felt embarrassed and far too conspicuous. Drawing attention to myself was not my style. At least not at a time of day when all I wanted was to shave my chin and drink my coffee—but that had spilled all over the floor.

Alas, even my new-found police friends could not get me there in time. Lewis had died just minutes before I arrived, and Caroline was inconsolable. She looked a fright as she stood there in her crumpled red dress, black runnels of mascara down her cheeks, and tangles of hair in disarray. Her despair was overwhelming and possibly contagious.

"What am I going to tell the children?" she sobbed as she hung on to me. "What's going to happen to me? Jerry, tell me; you must tell me!" A long, low moaning wail broke from her, and she fumbled for a Kleenex. "Lewis was all I had. I lived for him, and he lived for me. Why couldn't it have been someone else?"

I shook my head. I had no answer to that question.

I was speechless with grief. Lewis was one of those unusual people you cannot help loving. He was quiet and plump and a person whose friendship I appreciate more now than in his lifetime. He was selfless and utterly unassuming—a rare breed. I had been thankful for his intervention in meetings when he had graciously intercepted barbs that were maliciously aimed at me by those who felt called by God to bully the pastor. Worse still, he was almost exactly my age.

As I held his widow, I wished I could have had just a few minutes to thank him for all he had done for me. But I had been too self-consumed and reticent to do so. He may not have heard, but I would have probably felt a little better.

There was already a gap in my life that I would experience more acutely as time passed, and Lewis was not there to inject his friendly, civil, and selfless self. As my personal crisis deepened, I was going to need all the friends I could get. Now one I dearly needed was beyond my reach. That dreadful Saturday I grieved more for myself than for his widow.

*   *   *

In early fall the second crisis hit. This time it was Henry and Rebecca Chew. One Sunday morning Rebecca was in church alone. She was beautifully groomed as usual, but underneath the skillfully applied cosmetics she looked haggard.

Shaking my hand at the door she whispered, "Henry's gone. He's moved to Los Angeles, and I think he's taken another woman with him."

This blow sent me reeling. I had attempted to help this couple save their marriage. It seemed that I had failed, so I started to blame myself. Henry and Rebecca had been wonderful friends. I felt as if I had let them down.

All I wanted was personal space, but I had been programed to pour myself out for others. So I asked her to go and sit in my office, and I would be there when everyone had dispersed to the coffee hour.

It was forty-five minutes later that I managed to get to her. That wet, miserable morning everyone seemed to have a gripe. The rain had not ceased for days, bad weather making both young and old bad tempered. Instead of standing up for himself, the rector (in the person of myself) had allowed

61

himself to become the whipping boy and scapegoat of their wrath.

The older folks complained vociferously about the noise the kids made in church, while the young families moaned that there had not been enough help in the nursery. Still others niggled about the service, and the organist had stalked out of the building looking like a thundercloud for some reason unbeknown to anyone but himself.

I watched while one particularly obnoxious person positioned himself to drop a bomb on me. As I saw him coming toward me in the line, I knew World War III was about to begin. Shaking my hand vigorously, he started on me, his booming voice ensuring that the whole world would overhear his comments.

"I don't want to sound critical, Rector, but I want to tell you something—in the Lord, of course." This final proviso meant I was about to be damned to a thousand years in purgatory at least! "Your sermons have not been up to par recently. You know, we called you to be our rector because of your preaching; I'm not sure that we are getting our money's worth."

I wanted to lash out at the so-and-so. Behind my back I was clenching and unclenching my fist. My knuckles were white as I smiled charmingly and told him that I had been having a difficult few weeks, and besides, my salary was hardly princely.

"Wish I had the luxury of being able to have difficult weeks. If I didn't perform at work, they would probably get rid of me."

Before I could reply, he went off sanctimoniously to find a cup of coffee and, no doubt, share his misgivings about the Reverend Jeremy Wilkinson with his cronies in the parish hall. How I hated him. Had he no sensitivity? Couldn't he see I was in trouble?

Probably not. For years I had hidden the real me behind a mask that the congregation expected me to wear. The real me was worm-eaten and bitter, and I wondered whether Jesus Christ was worth so much trouble. Yet on the surface people saw a friendly pastor with a controlled temper, a loving smile, and an apparently infinite capacity to be trampled over without turning a hair.

I had almost forgotten Rebecca, so she heard me muttering uncharacteristic obscenities under my breath as I dragged my weary frame into my office and slammed the door.

"Jerry?" she said. I was startled and embarrassed at what she had overheard. Remembering why she was there, I started to apologize for being so tardy and for my unruly tongue.

"I'm sorry, Becca; I've had a lousy morning. There are some people in this congregation who would fray the nerves of angels, archangels, and all the company of heaven. They are driving me to distraction."

"Jerry, dear, they drove you there ages ago. I've been watching it happen. I know how unhappy you are. Since that little incident with your car in the summer the pounds have been dropping from you. If you were mine, I would be doing all I could to build you up again."

"Thanks for those encouraging words. I needed them," I said aloud. Inside myself I said, "She cares about me, and no one else seems to. How long has it been since Rachel called me 'dear'?"

"You don't want to know my troubles, though," I began. "What's all this about you and Henry?"

"Jerry, the worst mistake we ever made was to decide to have no children."

"Oh, I didn't know you. . . . I thought . . . I thought. . . ."

"You thought we couldn't. Is that what you are trying to say?"

"Yes, something like that."

"We could have had a quiverful if we wanted, but both of us, coming from broken homes, were frightened by the idea. Anyhow, Henry longed to make it to the top of the corporate totem pole, and I wanted to do all I could to help him get there. Besides, babies are a terrible responsibility."

I thought that perhaps this attitude explained why I had always known there was a sort of teenage immaturity about

Rebecca. But she always presented herself with such sophistication that I tended to discount it. She was a person who found it hard to cope with the inevitable restraints of adulthood. In retrospect I can see that I gave her far more than the benefit of the doubt.

"What has this to do with him leaving for Los Angeles?" I ventured.

"On Friday when I got home from work, his things were gone from the house. There was a note on the kitchen table telling me that he had been transferred to the California office at his own request and that he didn't want me to come with him."

Misery enshrouded her face as she repeated, "He didn't want me with him. Jerry, I know he's not alone. I'm almost 100 percent certain there's another woman."

"How do you know?"

"Female intuition. And the slight smell of her cheap scent when he came in from a late session at the office."

There was silence. She ferreted in her purse for a tissue, I thought. Instead, out came a cigarette that she put to her lips and lit with a little gold lighter.

"I didn't know you smoked."

"Gave it up years ago, but the strain has been terrible. Well, you know, we've talked to you several times. I need these to calm my nerves. I'll be able to throw the habit once life has achieved equilibrium again."

The room began to fill with a cloud of blue smoke. My eyes started watering. I hate cigarette smoke and normally dislike having to watch people smoking, but as she sat there in the big armchair, there was something seductive about her. She could easily have stepped out of the advertisement: "You've come a long way, Baby."

"Frankly, Jerry," she went on, "I'm relieved it's over. The anticipation has been killing me. I've been expecting something for a while, but this has taken me by surprise. Now it looks as if I'm free to live my own life again. And you can be certain that I will. But first I have to untie the knot that binds me to that creep." Her voice had taken on a venomous tone.

64

"Oh, come on; you can't turn your back on matrimony just like that." I was angry with her now. "Aren't you going to try and reconcile with him? I don't think everything is lost."

"No, Jeremy, its finished. For several years it has been fading. I've dreaded this moment, but now that it is here, I'm not going to allow it to destroy me. I'm going to pick myself up and carry on with living."

We talked for a little longer, and then I suggested we should pray. The words did not come easily, because I could not help remembering that forbidden kiss. The "Amen" having been said, we caught one another's eyes as we looked up. Each knew the other to be thinking about the same incident.

She gathered her things together, then said, "Come on, Jeremy, don't be such an old prude; you enjoyed that stolen moment just as much as I did."

I stood there looking embarrassed and speechless. She smiled and leaned forward and stole another kiss. Then squeezing my hand she fumbled in her purse for her car keys, indicating that she was ready to go.

Only when she had left did I realize that she had already discarded her wedding ring. It would have been hard to miss that something in her demeanor that seemed to say, "Look out, world, here I come!" Or was she looking out for Jeremy Wilkinson? A trap had been set and, like many another pastor, I started nibbling at the poisoned bait.

When I arrived home, the first thing Rachel and I did was to have a first-class row. I had forgotten that she had cooked something special for lunch. I was so late that it was ruined. The children had eaten wieners and gone off to play with friends. Rachel went off in a sulk, and I found myself mentally comparing the two women—no prizes for guessing which one came out the winner.

So it went on. Lew's death. Henry on the phone from Los Angeles explaining everything away. Rebecca, one moment expressing the bitterness of the wronged wife, the next throwing off the obligations and restraints of marriage. Within days of Henry's departure she had engaged lawyers to begin divorce proceedings. Once they were at work, their tactics made her all the more distraught.

In the midst of this three-ring circus, Rachel and I escalated our miscommunication even more. The faultfinding of the parish complaint squad became all the more shrill, and my ability to withstand their bludgeoning was ebbing away.

Each time I visited Jonathan I found myself wondering aloud where it would all end. I wanted to make sense of the tangled web of the week's events, and he would allow me to do so. But without my being aware of it, I was being forced to dig deep so that I would eventually be brought face-to-face with my darker self.

I continued to lose weight at the rate of about three pounds a week. It was impossible to read a book. I would sit for hours in my office staring absently into space. I could not remember when I had last exercised a devotional life.

My imagination was working overtime. My thoughts continually strayed back to Rebecca. Despite her own difficulties, she always showed concern for me. Meanwhile it seemed that a great gulf was fixed between my wife and me. Rebecca Chew became the focus of my daydreams and fantasies. It was not long before I was thinking the unthinkable.

But by the grace of God, I was saved from myself.

7

I was totally infatuated with Rebecca Chew. It should have been obvious to even the least observant person. For months we had unwittingly been giving each other all sorts of hidden signals. These had been picked up and amplified. Now I felt my emotions becoming entangled with hers, whether I liked it or not.

With my work slowly wringing the life from me and the health of my marriage at an all-time low, I was desperate for affection and affirmation. In order to get my attention, Rebecca offered me what I needed.

Some evenings, instead of going straight home from a meeting or from a visit to the hospital, I would drop by and see her. We would chat and drink hot chocolate, and I would deceive myself that I was making a pastoral call. At first, whenever I left, we would brush cheeks in the socially acceptable manner. But later, mesmerized by the pleasure of her company, this harmless ritual soon developed romantic overtones.

Practicing this deception intensified my inward hurt. At Rebecca's insistence I kept our developing relationship from Jonathan when I visited him each week for counseling. But as my guilt grew, I could contain my secret no longer. During one particularly grueling session the whole lot poured out.

My friend sat back in his chair with a benign grin on his face, "I wondered how long it would take you to get around to telling me the whole story."

"You knew?"

"I had a pretty good idea," he muttered, as he took a swig of lukewarm coffee and puffed contentedly on his pipe. I wanted to vomit.

Now that the plug had been pried loose, it all poured out. In the following weeks Jonathan did not have to work very hard to help me explore the many complexities of my sexuality. To my surprise, I found myself revealing facts and fantasies buried for years about which I had never spoken to a living soul before. Uncomfortable truths surfaced. In my discomfort, like a wrestler, I tussled with the dormant adolescent in me—a seemingly harmless child until he leered. I was face-to-face with the dark side of my soul and disgusted by its sinister countenance.

There were days when I wanted to give up on counseling. Yet instinctively I knew there would be no healing until I was willing to turn my life inside out, even to the point of airing out the sexual conundrum that had begun to smell awful. The whole agony had to see the light of day.

I do not wish to malign Rebecca; she was and is a fine person. I am sorry that I can no longer count her among my friends. In many respects hers were the highest intentions, for she saw me in trouble and wanted to help. I had supported her in her own trials. Returning my friendship was certainly the least she could do in turn. Had both our lives been less ravaged, I am sure that we would have handled ourselves very differently.

Henry's departure had left Rebecca lonely, short of money, and scared. Worst of all, by leaving her, he had robbed her of dignity and self-esteem. A warm, caring, affectionate person, she offered me what I craved but for some reason could not accept from my own wife at that juncture in my life. The explosion was inevitable.

So there we were—two needy people becoming increasingly dependent upon each other for emotional support. There was nothing smutty about our relationship, but I continue to wonder why I allowed myself to fall into the sort of trap that I had assiduously avoided on several occasions in the past. However, in retrospect, I have a much better understanding of St. Francis of Assisi's logic behind his refusal to allow himself the luxury of looking at a woman.

Human sexuality is a more powerful force than we ever imagine, and pastors find themselves in a steady stream of situations that could be compromising. We deal with members of the opposite sex at times in their lives when their emotions are most fragile. We are on call twenty-four hours a day, and we do not have the protection of a clinical environment and the fifty-minute counseling hour.

Prior to this episode I scorned clergy who sought solace with other women. Now I found myself being relentlessly dragged down the same road. I guess there is nothing unusual about what was happening; the problem is as old as the ordained ministry itself. It worried me immensely, yet I was reaching a point when I did not really care. Rebecca was turning into something special. All I wanted was for the sickening sense of guilt to go away. Perhaps then I could enjoy this "forbidden fruit."

Sleepless nights begat sleepless nights. My body yearned for rest, but with heart pounding and stomach muscles taut, I was incapable of more than odd hours of restless stupor. I would listen to Rachel's gentle breathing as she lay beside me and wonder why she had not blown the whistle on me. Her very silence betrayed her inner agony, but she suffered in silence.

I was confused, and I wished that I could feel something for her, but Rebecca always loomed larger in my feverish thoughts. In the darkness I would idealize her, always at Rachel's expense. She seemed to be everything I had always wanted, yet my Christian morality placed her beyond my reach.

On the other hand, the woman with whom I had spent so many years seemed a stranger. Looking back, my attitude toward my wife is hardly surprising. I had overindulged myself in ministry. I had organized my every waking hour around the church. When it was not the parish, it was the life of the diocese. Evenings were crammed with meetings; weekends were packed full of conferences, worship, sermon

69

preparation, and so forth. And there were always people coming and going.

My family had of necessity been relegated to second place, and Rachel had acquiesced to this arrangement. Many an evening I had been at dinner with my family in body only. In reality I was miles away puzzling over someone else's crisis. Despite repeated warnings in clergy journals and continuing education courses, I did not believe that this preoccupation with ministry would harm *my* home life. Other, weaker individuals, perhaps, but not *me*.

In my absence Rachel willingly shouldered a double load of parental responsibility. I was busy with the Lord's work, and she was my helpmeet, wasn't she? In addition, she tried hard to be a model rector's wife. Nevertheless, it was inevitable that her life should revolve around the children. With three young lives dependent upon her, she poured all her love into them, and they responded eagerly. Where else could she find the love that I foolishly withheld from her while I was away, ostensibly crusading for Christ but actually feeding my hungry ego?

Inevitably, as I compared the two women, Rachel came off badly. Rebecca had a flair for self-indulgence and was always immaculate. By comparison, Rachel was beginning to look dowdy and distinctly middle-aged. She did nothing to disguise the gray of her hair and would happily forego a dress for herself if Jeremy Junior needed new sneakers.

Sitting at the breakfast table I would covertly watch her and ask, "Can I bear to spend the rest of my life with a wife like her? She is bad enough now; what will she be like when she is sixty?"

Fool that I was, I applied the wrong standards to Rachel and was unwilling to shine the same demanding spotlight on Rebecca. To my deluded senses the two women were not even in the same class. My imagination ran wild, and I plotted absurd scenarios that removed my wife from the picture. Rebecca looked like the solution to all my problems.

"Perhaps in our day and age, when couples are expected to

stay together forty or fifty years, there is justification for making a change at midlife," I found myself musing.

So I went off to find people who would endorse my "revisionist" thinking. In a city like Boston one does not have to go too far to find such people, either within or outside the church.

Over lunch one day a minister of another denomination said to me, "I find traditional ethical mores inadequate in our time. I would go so far as to say that we must regard the recent findings of the social sciences as a continuation of divine revelation."

He was a man whose friendship and compassion I had always appreciated and respected, so such a statement was music to my ears. Yet as much as I tried to persuade myself that it would be all right to leave the wife to whom I had covenanted myself "until death us do part," the more I realized that my conscience had been too deeply impregnated by the imperative of God's words to allow such license without a bitter struggle.

The ethical agony was excruciating. Although my philandering was tame by twentieth-century standards, I expected the highest of myself, and in my own eyes I was becoming a hopeless womanizer. Far from bringing happiness, it merely multiplied my distress.

Then God intervened.

One morning I was at home trying to read the newspaper. These days, because I felt like a hypocrite, it was close to impossible for me to spend much time at the church. My heart would pound as I walked up the path or as I looked at the icon of Christ that hung in the sanctuary. Wherever I moved the eyes seemed to follow. I wanted to say, "Is it I, Lord?" I *knew* how Judas Iscariot must have felt on that night that sealed his fate, making himself the byword for treachery down through the ages.

Despite my faltering faith, Jesus would *not* let me go. I could fool my congregation, I thought I was fooling my wife, but I would never be able to pull the wool over *his* eyes.

So I pretended to my secretary and colleagues alike that I

71

was working in my study at home. "Work" had turned into a listless shuffling of papers and hours of nothingness. When I knew Rachel would be out of the house, I would call Rebecca and chat. By this stage such conversations were little more than tirades against virtually every fixed point in my life.

On this particular morning the phone rang, and I expected that familiar female voice at the other end of the line. Instead there was the click of a long-distance connection, and one of my oldest friends, pastor of a large Presbyterian church in the Chicago area, was talking to me.

"Hello, old buddy, how's tricks?" he said with forced affability.

"Pretty dreadful," I replied with all the honesty I could muster.

"What's up?"

"I think I'm. . . . I seem to be coming to pieces."

Then he dropped his guard. "You too?"

"Why, what's up with you?"

"Things are bad. Couldn't be worse. . . ." There was a long pause, and I wondered if we had been disconnected.

"Hello. Are you still there?" I questioned.

"Yes, I'm still here. I can't find the right words to tell you about it."

"Tell me about what?"

There was silence again. My heart was pounding. I had a premonition that I knew what he was going to say. I cleared my throat and, trying to sound casual, asked a second time, "What's up?"

There was yet another silence. Then out it all flowed: a mangled, garbled torrent of words. It would appear that he had been fired. His session had given him a generous severance, but he had suddenly turned into the black sheep of the presbytery and felt he would never be able to get another position in a Presbyterian church.

"Oh, come on. That can't be true!" I interjected. I am not sure that he even heard my words. For ten or fifteen minutes he ranted on, but I knew he was walking around the real problem.

72

Like so many clergy, his ordination ceremony was the day on which he married the church. He was a fine pastor and a profound preacher. He seemed to succeed with little effort at all that he did. Quickly he found his way into the pulpit of a prestigious and influential congregation, and it seemed that everything he touched turned to gold. He had a beautiful wife, a pair of delightful sons, and a lovely home.

"But you know, old buddy," he pondered, "I had gotten to the point where I found it impossible to drag myself out of bed each morning. All I wanted was peace, quiet, and a life of my own."

Then "this woman" appeared on the scene. With those words, my heart stopped. I now knew what he was going to tell me, and I wanted to hear no more. But I was scared to interrupt the story and hoped that it would take a different tack.

She was a divorcée. Attractive and alone, she had moved from the East and affiliated with his congregation. A gifted teacher, she had quickly involved herself in the Sunday school, and Kenneth soon found himself relying on her sound judgment and good sense. When he had a Christian education decision, he depended on her advice.

As the relationship developed, he discovered his motives were far from pure. He tried to make a break and could not. The friendship blossomed in unforeseen directions, and he threw caution to the wind. He left his wife and rented an apartment but spent most of his time at this woman's home. This was when the session blew the whistle on him.

It took no more than a few weeks for the relationship to turn sour, but the damage had been done. Now he was alone, living in a seedy rented room; the apartment had turned out to be too expensive. He was working in the men's department of a local store owned by a member of the church who had taken pity on him.

"How did it happen?" I kept appealing. He did not hear my requests, wrapped up as he was in his own demise. When eventually he did answer, the only words he seemed able to say were, "Honestly, I don't know. I must have suffered some kind of midlife madness or something."

"Will you go back to Denise?"

"She won't have me. In fact, she is so mad at me that she has been trying to get a legal injunction to stop me from seeing the kids. Man, I'm forty-four, and I'm finished. God, I'd give anything to put the clock back eight or nine months and remake some poor decisions."

By now he was weeping at the other end of the line. Long, low sobs, muffled by a handkerchief came down the receiver toward me. I was at a loss to know what to say. Things must have reached a pretty terrible pass for so sweet a woman as Denise McDermott to cut her erring husband out of her life so violently.

"Do you want to go back to Denise?" I questioned after waiting what seemed like an eternity for him to say something.

"Old buddy, I'm not sure. The last few years together have been pretty terrible. We just didn't seem to have anything left in common. Frankly, I used to stay late at church in order to avoid another battle at home. That's how I found myself getting entangled with Eloise."

Again there was a silence at the end of the line. Then once more he spoke. "All my energy was poured into nurturing the congregation. Denise and I just did not seem to have time for one another anymore. It wasn't all my fault though: she developed a passion to belong to all the right women's gatherings. I've gotten fed up with being her consort at committees to support the symphony and the Junior League."

There was silence again. Then, "She is history and so is my ministry. I've had it with the church."

I encouraged him to talk on. "Whatever I tried, all *they* could do was throw it back in my face. And that wife of mine sided with my detractors. She's been carrying on like all those smug, self-satisfied pew warmers there. She says, 'I'll have you back under this roof only if you come back under my terms.' God, I hate Presbyterians; you Episcopalians are much more tolerant and compassionate."

I tried to say something to the contrary, but the words were flowing in torrents again.

"Old buddy, I've spent half my life on this planet living by her terms; now she must listen to mine." On the tirade went. He seemed to be thinking aloud and was being hopelessly unfair to his spouse. She had supported him through seminary and had gone without, sacrificing her own promising career so that he might be the pastor he had become.

I remonstrated with him, but the conversation was going nowhere.

"How ironic," I was thinking, "Here I am saying things to him that I know I should be saying to myself: 'Physician, heal thyself!'"

At last the conversation dried up, he gave me his phone number, and we hung up. I have not talked with Kenneth since. Somehow it was as if he had called to say goodbye to me. Our lives have taken radically different courses. Soon he was managing the men's department at that store; then I heard that he had gone into business on his own. He is very gifted; I expect he will make a go of it.

Denise and Kenneth are now divorced, and she has moved to Florida where she is teaching in the Tampa area. I would be hard-pressed to know where to get in touch with Ken today. I guess he is just one of thousands of ex-pastors who have missed the mark and are now working hard to live down their ministerial past.

After Ken's call, I found myself wandering distractedly around the house murmuring at intervals, "There but for the grace of God go I." I might have been saying the words, but I was having great trouble believing that God even existed.

Ken's story was a real warning. I knew at all costs that I must tear myself away from Rebecca and her siren-like charms, but how should I go about it? For the last few months she was just about all that had kept me afloat. If I didn't act, God knows what would happen to me. If I did, what was there left worth living for? Racking my brain, I could not answer that question.

I suppose I date my entry into the darkest section of this tunnel of despair to that conversation. There was no light at its end.

"Good grief," I said to myself, "I do not want to take Kenneth's route, but then without Rebecca what is there to live for?"

What was God up to? He seemed to have abandoned me to wallow in my own filth. The heavens were closed to my pleas. For the remainder of the day I wandered around listlessly doing just a handful of those pastoral jobs that were essential to prevent the church from completely falling apart.

I talked to a couple about the baptism of their child. As they cooed over the infant gurgling in the crib and looked lovingly into each other's eyes, I cynically wondered how long it would be before their relationship began to unravel. I envied them in their marital bliss, but in my anguished state I could only translate that envy into a variety of mild disgust.

When night had fallen I excused myself from responsibilities at church and home and headed for one of my favorite haunts overlooking the ocean. Leaving the car, I stood looking out toward the horizon. The wind seemed to slice me in half as I walked the beach, and the eternal rhythm of the ocean sounded in my ears like the drums of the worshipers of some primitive deity, enthusiastically scorning my very existence.

The stars shone. They assured me that the God who had made and kept a promise to Abraham and Sarah cared about me also. But I was too angry to perceive their twinkling eloquence. There I stood like Søren Kierkegaard and railed against God, shaking my fist at a heaven that I wanted to believe was empty and Godless. Yet I would have been terrified out of my wits had that been true.

"There is no God," I blubbered. "If there were, he would do something about the misery of life. I'm halfway through my allotted span, and I'm married to the wrong woman and see no way out of the stranglehold. I've been so conditioned by an outmoded set of values that I cannot bring myself to throw them overboard. Have I given the best years of my life to a mirage?"

A plan was forming in my mind. I would go to California. There I could make a fresh start. I would leave Rachel and Rebecca behind. Best of all, I would leave the church. If something dreadful happened to me, let them wallow in guilt, wondering what they had contributed to the disaster. Only by beginning again would I be able to make something of the years that remained.

This wasn't running away, I tried to persuade myself. This was a prudent exit from an impossible situation. Like the hippies of the sixties, I was going somewhere to reinvent myself. If I started again from the beginning, I could make a different set of decisions in light of my present knowledge. I could forget I had ever been a priest, a servant of the Most High God. The only element of my escape that upset me was the prospect of leaving my children behind.

I walked on with my hands thrust deep into my coat pockets. Just to have made a decision felt good, but would I have the courage to go through with it? My thoughts turned once more to those members at St. Mary's who had been a thorn in my side.

"Damn the lot of them," I screamed to the restless waves. "I don't care a jot about what happens to them or to me. . . . And as for that counselor, I've wasted a fortune, and it hasn't done me much good." But here was the rub: I really *did* care, and I cared much more than a jot. To quote Kipling, I cared "with all my heart and nerve and sinew"! The last thing in the world that I wanted was to make shipwreck of my life, but what options were there left open? And God? I reopened the debate on his existence convinced that he did not love me. I knew it took more than a well-contrived fairy tale to claim so many lives and allegiances through history, but for the moment, the power of the gospel message was elusive.

By this stage I was talking hard. If I stopped I might rediscover that God was more than a figment of an overripe imagination, and I'm not sure I wanted that at this point.

With my conscious mind I dismissed him, but deep within and unbeknown to me, he was still at work.

At this point it would have been easy for me to think that it was the Almighty's plan for me to reach this point of disintegration. Were this true, I would have turned him into a tyrant and myself into a robot. Certainly he worked through these awful experiences to bring me to myself, but I alone was to blame for my state of affairs. Only in coming apart was it possible for me to see a healing process begin.

I was adrift on the sea of life—a sea like "Dover Beach," with a "melancholy, long, withdrawing roar." But maybe something significant happened that night of which I will never be fully aware.

8

The days that followed that evening on the beach are little more than a blur of hazy recollections, with only occasional highlights making a lasting impression on my mind. I was in excruciating psychological pain: an emotional boil was about to burst. I was sensing a signal that time had run out. I was intensely uncomfortable. My nerve was broken. I knew something precipitative would happen.

If I give the impression that anything was premeditated, forgive me. So much happened on the spur of the moment. For several days I was so controlled by my brutalized feelings that I followed their lead, giving little thought to the consequence of my actions. Friends and associates will tell you this was completely out of character: my life is normally well planned and fairly orderly.

But then almost everything that took place during this time did not fit with the face I had showed the world for so long. In many respects I became a stranger to those who knew me best and to myself a frightening enigma. My world seemed to be fragmenting. Worse still, I knew I was the cause of the mayhem.

The term "ministerial burnout" is used to describe the effects of emotional and spiritual overload. To me this is an inadequate description of something so complex and so extraordinarily agonizing. I felt burned up not burned out, and the damage had been done less by fire than by a creeping frosty death that spread its tentacles from someplace deep inside outward to my whole being.

Coming home from the shore, I slept no better than usual. Rachel's pretended slumber was also restless. Perhaps she was aware that something dreadful was about to shatter her carefully constructed world. The next day began as every other for as long as I could remember: a sickening cloud of gloom and emptiness hung over me from the moment I opened my eyes.

Physically all I felt good for was to vomit. Half-heartedly I attempted to do some work. The next Sunday I was going to preach, but as I looked at the lectionary readings they seemed so much jibberish. What should I say? What *could* I say? The only response I could find was, "Nothing."

I wanted to get into the pulpit and ask the congregation to be patient with me because I was having profound doubts about my faith. If God was not dead, then as far as I could see he was in a state of terminal ill health. "Give me space," I wanted to scream.

I found it impossible to concentrate on the words before me. Instead, my imagination went to work on the shocked expressions that would spread across the faces there in the pews if I gave such a performance. Involuntarily, I treated myself to the luxury of a malignant grin. I felt that they would never let me get away with such honesty. Besides, more was amiss than just that.

Since the day of my ordination the pulpit had always been important to me, and I find its misuse disconcerting. For me it is a sacred setting from which profound facts of faith are affirmed. Even in the midst of personal turmoil I could not justify misusing it, perhaps doing lasting damage to individuals committed to my charge.

I would rather never peach again than not preach properly. I had reached a crossroads and knew which way I should not go. Under no circumstances could I ascend those steps on Sunday.

Going into the kitchen, I poured a cup of coffee and took a sip. Like most food and drink during these months, it left me feeling sick to my stomach. I sat to think and let it go cold. As I turned to leave, I caught sight of myself in a mirror. I

80

looked pale, gaunt, malnourished, and weary. The mirror brought me face-to-face with an undeniable truth.

Heading back to the study, I sat down and fumbled with my pen. My heart pounded as I set about writing two notes: one to Rachel, the other to Rebecca.

In the first, I told my wife that it was no use to keep working on our marriage. I was going away and would be in touch with her when I had come to grips with myself. I coldly asserted that our marriage was in such a state of disrepair that it was beyond resurrection.

"We may as well give up on it and go our separate ways. I have had grave doubts about our relationship for a long time. You probably love me, but I am not sure I love you. I wonder whether I ever have. You're a good woman, and you deserve a great deal better than I can ever give."

That very morning we had had a misunderstanding. We *always* seemed to be talking at cross-purposes these days. A scene ensued in which I deliberately set out to hurt her. Perhaps I wanted her to say, "Jeremy Wilkinson, you're a dead loss. Get out of my life. I never want to see you again." That would have suited me just fine. At least, that is what I tried to persuade myself.

The words now started to flow freely, "What is worse, my faith is in such tatters that I am forced to conclude that even if God exists, he cannot be worth loving. He seems little more than a cruel tyrant of the skies, laughing gleefully at poor mortals slithering and writhing their way through life—the victims of his whims. Job's wife was right, 'Curse God and die!' "

There was less bitterness in the second letter. I was not angry with Rebecca; I was just sorry that circumstances prevented our relationship from maturing. Even if she was up to an affair, which I very much doubted, I was not. I urged her to leave me alone and thanked her for the many ways in which she had tried to be of support and assistance during this intensely painful time. In my last paragraph to her, I became a pastor again just for a moment. Walking out on ministry does not break habits that have shaped a lifetime. I wrote, "Stop putting your life on hold and waiting for something that will never happen. I am no good for man, woman, child, or beast. You have much to offer the world that will give comfort to others and will make a contribution to this poor, benighted human race."

Going upstairs I grabbed an old suitcase, stuffed in a few clothes, a book, and a couple of sentimental knickknacks; then I looked around for the last time. Tears welled up as I poked my head into the children's rooms. I loved them dearly and was undone by the realization that they had been the victims of parish ministry, doomed always to live on the periphery of my life.

I would miss them very much. I felt guilty about my failures as a father. Reality had become so twisted that I believed the action I was taking was best for them. "They will be better off without me," I tried to convince myself. The longer I hung around, the worse off they would be, so I would depart and improve their lot.

Downstairs I made a pitstop in the bathroom just inside the front door. Coming out, I found myself face-to-face with Rachel, who was just arriving home from a trip to the supermarket. She was earlier than I had expected and caught me in midflight. I had bungled it. Since then I have often asked myself whether unconsciously I had actually wanted her to catch me.

In her hand was the note I had written. I had pinned it to the front door before slipping to the bathroom. To my dying day I will not forget the look of bewildered anguish on her face. For a second I relented and decided I loved her passionately, but it passed.

"Jeremy Wilkinson, what in God's name does *this* mean?" Her voice quivered with rising fear, anger, and hostility. She waved the scrappy piece of paper in my face. Her words were like the scream of a frightened animal, not the inquiry of a rational human being.

She continued: "Don't you think I've been sharing your agony for the past months? Do you realize how anxious and worried I have been for you? You've been running around like a puppy after that wretched Chew woman, and you've done everything to shut me out of your life." She stopped for breath, then her voice cracked as she whispered, "For God's sake, why? What have I done wrong? Why is this happening to us?"

We batted words to and fro, but neither seemed able to hear the other. Fumbling for words, I struggled to explain what I was doing, but the more I talked the less sense it made. At that moment Rachel thought I was committing spiritual suicide, and she was right.

We stood talking past one another, and in the same moment I found myself loving and hating her. If I had allowed love to prevail, how different things would have been, but I did not. Finally, in utter frustration she burst into tears and ran into the family room where she threw herself onto the sofa, pounding it as if to beat some sense into it.

I followed, still struggling to explain what I had in mind. The encounter was turning into a shouting match of epic proportions. She was sprawled across the cushions, her skirt hitched over her thighs, her face blotchy with tears, mascara-colored streams staining her cheeks.

Whenever she made a point that I could not counter, I would yell expletives like, "Oh, get off my back, woman!"

One of the problems of our relationship was that we had always been polite with one another. I was afraid to deal with the stresses on our marriage, because anything I said to Rachel was taken as implied criticism. A cold chill would descend over the household for days, so in the end I gave up and bottled it all in.

Now the door was opening, and the recriminations that had been filed for years came pouring out. This Pandora's box was going to be as difficult to close as that of mythology. As in the myth, every last "monster" that we had relegated to the subconscious of our marriage had to force its way out before we would find hope for ourselves.

Eventually the storm blew itself out. Then she spoke, softly this time, but with great command. "If you are leaving both me and the parish, it's your duty to tell the bishop you are resigning." That was a blow to the stomach that she followed immediately with, "You owe it to your parents, too. You must tell them what you are up to, or they will die with worry."

Another battle ensued. The bishop was well aware of the struggles I was having. I had visited him on several occasions and had been overwhelmed by his loving support. Rachel was right to insist that if I was about to leave, he had a right to know. My duties had to be taken over, and he had to find the right person to care for a congregation in transition.

"Oh, don't give me all that duty stuff. I've had it up to here with my duty," I yelled, signing with my hands that I was drowning. "I don't owe anybody anything." I ranted and raved because her second suggestion had made my blood boil. "But in order to keep you happy I will call the bishop's office. And I'll tell Mom and Dad the same things I've told you. Won't you all, for God's sake, get off my back."

Perhaps, without realizing it, Rachel had made a shrewd move. It came from a woman who knew me better than I realized and loved me more than I imagined. She was attempting to provide some containment for my rage, giving me an opportunity to catch my breath before taking off on an odyssey. Her intervention turned my intended geographical journey into an internal one.

*   *   *

I called the bishop's office first.

Let me tell you about our bishop. He is a wise and saintly man. He is always in great demand in our diocese, in the Episcopal church, and in Christendom. I have always marveled that a person of his age is able to squeeze so much into life. He was close to retirement but still achieved more in a day than a majority of clergy do in a week. I thank God that he was there when I came unthreaded.

When I got through to his secretary, I tried to sound casual, asking whether the bishop was in—hoping that the bishop was out.

"He has someone with him at the moment, Jeremy. Can I get him to call you back?"

"I don't know if I'll be here when he does."

She picked up something in my tone of voice. Helena's great skill is protecting her boss from unnecessary interruptions, but she has a sixth sense that enables her to recognize a problem that needs immediate episcopal attention.

"Hold on," she said, and a moment later I heard the voice of the Right Reverend Ian Rees on the line.

I started in, "Bishop, I'm finished. I want to resign immediately, and I'm leaving for the West Coast today. Rachel and the kids will stay here, but I must get away. I don't know where I'm going, but I've got to escape."

Bishop Rees usually leads by getting alongside a person rather than by issuing preemptive commands. I do not know what I expected when I spoke to him, but whatever it was, I was unprepared for the cold edge of authority in his reply.

"Jeremy, you are going nowhere. I have to be at one of the parishes on the Cape this evening, but I expect you in my office first thing in the morning. Oh, and bring Rachel with you."

"Yes, sir," I meekly replied, unable to argue.

"I will call your assistant and wardens and tell them you aren't well and need to be left alone for a while. Is that all right?"

The question was a rhetorical one. Before I could respond, he finished the conversation. "If you will allow me to return to the person in my office, I will see you in the morning at nine o'clock sharp." He paused, then speaking more gently said, "Oh, by the way, my friend, you can be sure that we will be praying for you."

By the time I hung up, my whole body was shaking. My legs gave out beneath me, and I crumbled into a heap on the carpet. It was as if a plug had been pulled out somewhere deep inside me. My eyes began filling with tears, and the next moment I was weeping uncontrollably.

Rachel came over and comforted me. I held onto her like a

child clinging to his mother's skirt on the first day of school. Mothering was what I needed, and Rachel knew what to do.

The next hours are a confusion. The phone kept ringing, and I was conscious of a whirl of activity around me. The children were diverted from school to a friend's home. To my surprise, by early evening I was sitting in Jonathan's office. Only this time it was not just the two of us; now there was Rachel and a psychiatrist as well.

I remember little of what happened while we were there, but I do know we were at the counseling center for the best part of three hours. On the way home we stopped by a pharmacy to pick up antidepressant drugs that the "shrink" had prescribed before leaving Jonathan and me alone.

That evening's conversation with Jonathan is lost to my memory. The day I will never forget was drawing to a close, but what we talked about, I cannot tell you. I do recall that he acted not just as a skilled therapist but also as a priest of the church, hearing my confession and pronouncing absolution in the name of the Almighty One.

*   *   *

At 9:00 in the morning we were in the bishop's office. From its windows one can look out across the rooftops of Beacon Hill toward the gold dome of the State House. Again, Rachel was at my side. Despite the fact that the bishop had insisted that Rachel come with me, I was feeling sullen and antagonistic toward her, and in addition, my head was throbbing. I mused that "Nanny" had come to keep an eye on me. I felt like an organ grinder's monkey on the end of a short chain. She had decided that I needed a keeper to prevent me from getting into any more trouble.

After hearing the whole story, the bishop decided I needed a leave of absence during which he would assist with the counseling fees. In the same authoritative manner with which he had handled me on the phone the previous afternoon, he insisted that Rachel be part of the counseling process also.

"You're in this together. Putting himself under too much

86

stress has gotten Jeremy to this point, but it takes two to get a marriage into such a state of disrepair. I dare say there is a great deal that you two need to unpack before you can pick up the reins of a relatively normal existence again."

Rachel was the model of obedience. Up to this point she had blamed me for most of our problems, but now she was beginning to recognize that we were in this together. Also, she was fighting for her marriage and was ready to do anything the bishop told her. She nodded demurely. Had she declined, I would probably be telling a very different story.

At the time, I was angry at his peremptory style. Now I can love the man for his toughness. As we walked out of his office, I knew I had been given my orders, and woe to me if I diverged one inch to either the left or the right.

Recently, the bishop and I have talked about that occasion. He is retired now, so we met for lunch at one of the little restaurants in the New England town in which he lives. When I asked why he had been so dictatorial, he told me that he instinctively knew that the only way he could get through to me was by behaving like a drill sergeant. "Jeremy, this was one of those few occasions on which I wished I had all the trappings of power of a prince-bishop of the medieval church. If you hadn't obeyed, I would have thrown you into the slammer!" We laughed, but I knew he wasn't kidding.

I got home from the bishop's office, knowing that he would take care of my parish. He was to talk to the lay leaders and staff. He would do all he could to help them handle the crisis that, overnight, was to have a major impact on the life of the congregation. He did it well. To my surprise the people were supportive and concerned for me. They gave all the help they could and inundated our home with cards and gifts. Often families would take our children out on little treats.

Behaving like a wounded animal, I retreated into my lair. I wanted to go nowhere and to see no one. I was even a little frightened of going out in the car in case I saw someone I knew and was forced to wave. I became a prisoner in my own home. The boil had burst, my life was in rags and tatters, but I no longer carried the responsibility of ministry. The peace was fragile, yet for the moment it was better than anything I had known for a very long time.

My bookshelves bear witness to the way I spent that time "underground." Each day I would sit reading paperback novels and thrillers. Over a period of two weeks I probably read more stories and gripping yarns than I had in the previous decade. My numb mind soaked them up like the ground greets the rain after a long period of drought.

Having been buried in theological tomes for so long, my imagination had thirsted to the point of death. Now it guzzled science fiction, mystery stories, whodunits, and historical novels. A monsoon washed in. At another level healing was taking place. The tales that others told were a soothing balm that provided a kind of protective coating for my emotions and my inner being.

Apart from trips out for counseling, returning home via a bookstore where I stocked up for the next chapter of siege, I would dare creep out only in the dead of night and walk the deserted streets, hoping that I would not meet someone I knew. Confusion and shame controlled me. The more they terrorized me, the more necessary it became for me to escape into the novelists' make-believe world.

I hated the reality I knew I had to confront. Even in Jonathan's office I sometimes refused to face up to what was happening. As I mentioned before, much of this period is a blur in my mind, but I remember well that in the face of this insurmountable obstacle Alice came to the rescue.

Alice appeared earlier in my story, but you may not remember her. A sprightly widow, she had become aware of my discomfort months before the crisis erupted. She had gradually opened me up. She was the one person at St. Mary's in whom I felt I could confide, and it did not take her long to get to know me inside out. At the start of my leave of absence, I kept out of her way like everyone else. I think I probably resented her for much the same reason that I resented Jonathan: both of them knew me too well.

Later I was to learn that the week after I went into my hole she had called my counselor and asked how she might be of assistance. He had suggested that she try to coax me out. She waited until a crisp sunny day, then called and invited me to go walking with her.

"It will do you good, Jeremy," she insisted, but I refused to go.

Alice is a patient and not easily deflected soul. Day after day she called back until, at last, I relented. We had gone walking before my attempted "great escape." Now she saw to it that this became a daily habit. Off we would go for several hours each morning, and often I would eat a light lunch with her. This gave Rachel some respite from the mounting tension of having me around the house.

Whether beside the ocean or through the woods—wherever we walked—Alice listened and I talked. I fumed about everything under the sun. Only as I think about it now do I remember the little comments that this wise woman made, gently nudging me back toward balance and sanity.

Two issues dominated my thinking. With my faith in such tatters, could I go back to parish ministry—now or ever? And was my marriage heading for dissolution, making my children the offspring of a broken home? These problems nagged at me. Imperceptibly they were moving toward resolution, but from inside it felt as if we were going round and round in ever-decreasing circles.

9

News of my demise reached colleagues in ministry on the ubiquitous grapevine. A few called; many more wrote notes. Most of them were supportive and caring. A handful weighed me in the balances and found me wanting. Every few days the bishop would be in touch. I was comforted by his concern.

One Sunday a Pentecostal pastor who was little more than a passing acquaintance dropped by after his evening service. I was touched by his interest in me and opened up to him a tad. Even one of the rabbis let me know that he was adding me to his prayer list.

In the time since my recovery, I have wondered what it must be like to burn out and not have the support of fellow clergy. The love and sensitivity of ordained men and women was a soothing balm during those troubled times. I am sorry it took me so long to discover how many friends I really had. I wish I had been more open to their support sooner.

Because they were under similar pressures, clergy friends knew the kind of burden I was carrying—that it could trigger a precipitous decline. They were able to empathize with the victim. There were only a handful of detractors. I am inclined to believe that their inability to treat me compassionately was stimulated by the fear of a similar cauldron churning inside themselves. Or perhaps they were totally oblivious to the stresses of the pastoral ministry.

Several weeks after I had gone into my hole, my clergy friends began digging me out. The phone might ring and somebody would offer an invitation to lunch. Initially these were frightening occasions—I felt as if every eye in the restaurant was fixed on me. But gradually my composure started to return, even if I ate very little.

One friend insisted on dragging me out to play a late-season game of golf. I put the ball everywhere except the fairways and greens, but it was good to be out even if I was playing like a rank beginner. An Episcopal woman priest made herself my honorary "big sister." Some of the older clergy who had seen guys blow up before or had gone through a similar dark valley themselves gently shared their experience with me or became sounding boards as I wrestled with my problems.

For many weeks on Thursday I would lunch with Brian. He ate and I nibbled at Alphonso's diner in Revere. Despite this opportunity to be exposed regularly to Alphonso's individualistic rendering of the English language, I still failed to understand half the words he spoke! Brian had been right to encourage me to see Jonathan for professional counseling. But because being a pastor is in his blood, his listening ear became an important adjunct to the therapy I was undergoing.

Counseling sessions were unpredictable. Sometimes, as if from nowhere, great waves of emotion would well up inside me. Ambiguities emerged with which I would have to struggle: how could I be such an enigmatic mixture of good and evil? What sense could I make of the need I had for Rachel's love and intimacy, while at the same time needing "space" to find myself? Was it possible for me to change horses and leave the pastoral ministry in the middle of my career? While Jonathan kept me working on myself, the side effects of these emotional outpourings would leave me totally wrung out. He would smile and launch into his usual wrap-ups.

"Well, let's leave it there. We've done some good work this week. Now, can you make it at the same time next Wednesday?"

Often I would want to bellow. "No, you sadist, I don't even want to see you again." But I did not. I would nod, make a mental note of the appointment, grab my coat, and head for the parking lot before too many people could see me. Often my destination would be my bed—to sleep, perchance to dream.

By the time I was granted a leave of absence, I had reached that point in the therapy process where I had become extraordinarily dependent upon Jonathan. Despite my occasional feelings of animosity toward him, ruefully I would wonder how I was going to manage until our next session.

I depended on those sessions like an addictive drug. When things were going particularly badly, Jonathan would fit in extra emergency appointments. I found it impossible to function without him. I wanted him to play a vital part in the management of my life, and I wondered whether I would ever regain my autonomy.

The simplest decisions were transformed into impossible obstacle courses. I must have tried every trick in the book to get Jonathan to make them for me. He refused to take that kind of responsibility. He provided the back-up that I needed, and he helped me examine my motives and take a look at the subconscious realities in my life; but however much I tried, he stubbornly bucked every effort I made to push him into the driver's seat.

Even then I knew that if he had allowed himself to take over decision making for the confused and uncertain piece of humanity that dragged itself into his office, I would never have dealt with the two big issues that were staring me in the face: my ministry and my marriage.

After the initial whirlwind had passed, my extreme negativity toward the church began to wane. Now that I was in *real trouble*, the church was coming through in so many positive ways that I was forced to revise my pessimistic assessments of the summer. The bishop was treating me in a princely manner, my colleagues were rooting for me, and, with the exception of all but the most intransigent in the parish, my congregation was reaching out to soothe our wounds: mine and Rachel's.

There were days when I would wander restlessly around

the house pondering my circumstances. I was convinced that I was an idiot who had made a complete fool of himself and whose sanity had left him forever. When these thoughts surfaced, I would find myself staring into the frightened abyss again. Although I was never suicidal, I wondered whether the effort to keep going was really worth it. Since this happened to me, I have met burned-out clergy who have seriously considered taking their own lives.

Rachel would attempt to encourage me along. Unlike Jonathan, she seemed unable to prevent herself from taking over my life, so she would hover around like a brooding hen with a troublesome chick. Customarily our joint counseling sessions would turn into pitched battles. Instead of using physical objects as weapons, we used words—words that were subtle, cunning, and venomous.

Each of us further poisoned the relationship in our own way. Rachel smothered it with misdirected love. I changed the rules of our internal squabbles and put her down at every opportunity. Wistfully I would remind her that she would never, in a thousand years, match up to all that Rebecca had tried to be for me. Occasionally Rebecca would call. Talking with her presented me with a tremendous temptation to ignite the flame again, but somehow I managed to resist.

My wife is a shrewd and stubborn woman. There are times when she demonstrates how much better she knows me than I know myself. Inevitably her probings would get too close, and I would turn and run. I refused to allow her to claim any ownership of what might be tearing me apart. I wanted to keep my demons to myself. Even if it wounded her, I would find ways to escape her clutches.

In our counseling sessions, we acted out with terrifying intensity the antagonisms that had remained hidden for years. The equilibrium of normal home life was gone; this was the championship fight—so neither of us pulled any punches. As we approached the final rounds, I realized that Rachel perceived me to be a tiresome little boy and that her mission was to subdue me.

I started severing the ties that had bound us for so long.

94

"I am your thrall," I would rage. "I am determined to break the shackles that keep me under your thumb."

I took to sleeping in the spare bedroom. I opened a separate bank account for myself. Now that I was feeling less frightened by the outside world, I came and went as I pleased. She unwittingly played the part of scapegoat onto whom I loaded my woes and shortcomings.

Alice monitored the progress of this civil war. She understood that things would deteriorate before they started improving again. One day at lunch, quite out of the blue, she showed me the third floor of her large and elegant home.

"This place is too big for me, Jeremy. I would be happy to offer you bed and board if it becomes too difficult for you and Rachel to remain under the same roof. I'm not offering it as a permanent arrangement, you understand, but just to give you both some space."

I was taken aback by her generosity. Until this point I had envisioned Rachel and me slugging it out into the indefinite future, living separately but under the same roof because we could afford nothing else. That prospect was intolerable. During the following days this new escape route looked eminently attractive.

No more Rachel. No more tension. No more being kicked around by a woman for whom, to my deluded mind, I seemed little more than a meal ticket. But what about my children? Could I leave them with her? I shuddered at the thought but recognized that there was little I could do about that. When our case reached the courts, it was highly likely that she would be made the custodial parent, so I may as well get used to the idea.

My kids had become vitally important to me; they seemed to be all I had left. My leave of absence was allowing me to spend more time with them. I went to parent-teacher meetings. I helped them with their homework. I took them out to eat ice cream, and we fooled around on our home computer. For the first time in my adult life I had evenings at home. I was starting to learn to be a practicing father rather than a wraith who lives at the church, coming and going as ecclesiastical responsibilities allowed.

Because of the strained relationship between their mother and me, I poured my hungry love all over my children. I did this because I was discovering how much I appreciated being part of their lives. But I must admit that some of the attention they received was motivated by competition. I wanted them to love me more than they loved Rachel. So, in subtle ways, I put pressure on them. That they were living in a war zone was hard enough. That their parents should compete over them made matters even worse. Their lives reflected the disorientation.

A pastor's ministry and marriage are an integral part of one another. I was coming to the conclusion that separation would be the best thing for all concerned. I knew that if our marriage came unglued, the possibility of my remaining in ministry would be remote. The people at St. Mary's were unlikely to consider a divorced man a suitable rector.

Anyhow, as I could see no way to mend the tattered remnants of my faith at that point, I doubted that I could continue in that role. I no longer wanted to minister. I had little to say to them and loathed the impositions they placed upon me. The more cynical aspects of my disbelief were diminishing, but the framework of belief with which I had lived for two decades needed reconstruction. My struggle forced me back to the foundation to work through aspects of the Christian message that I thought I had mastered years before.

By this stage antidepressants were buoying me up and sheltering me from the pain that should normally accompany such a radical reassessment of the past. Certainly, this chemical therapy was helpful, but I wonder whether I would have been quite such a revolutionary had I been forced to wrestle with my decisions without this artificially induced emotional safety net.

On the other hand, without the help of medication, I might have done something far worse. Maybe I *would* have committed suicide or just disappeared, driving westward to California and, finding the Golden Gate Bridge, then what? These will always be "what if?" questions that I can never answer.

If Rachel and I separated, I would have to find myself another job. What would I do? Being a pastor gives a person a cross section of career skills, so I was convinced that it would not take long to find a lucrative position with some small corporation. In fact, all they needed to do was to see my resume, and they would hire me on the spot. How naïve I was!

I set to work looking for employment and discovered that fifteen years of pastoral ministry had equipped me to be only a pastor; potential employers thought that I was good for little else. The organizational, management, and "people" skills developed by a pastor were considered "soft" in the rough-and-tumble of the world of business and commerce.

If my marriage were to come completely unthreaded, I would have to find the funds to keep Rachel and the kids as well as myself. Yet whenever I pursued a position that required the sort of skills acquired as a parish priest, interviewers refused to take me seriously.

To my horror, I was finding out that however capable I might have been considered in the religious realm, secular organizations do not take church experience seriously. But I was learning the art of networking, and to my delight, I found I was pretty good at it. Before long I had an extraordinary web of relationships around Boston among human resources people, nonprofit managers, administrators, counselors, and people in publishing. I was sure that these would eventually yield the career opportunities that I wanted.

Two months of my leave of absence were spent job hunting. Christmas came and went, but there was still nothing on the horizon. I had set out optimistically, reckoning that it would take six or seven weeks to land something substantial. I ended up gravely disappointed, with my ego bruised even further. I was bloody but unbowed.

*   *   *

97

When it became clear that a secular job would take longer to materialize than I expected, I decided, with Jonathan's help, to go back to the parish. I would work at it as best I could and keep looking for employment while I still had a steady income and the rectory as a roof over my head. The people there might not like what they saw, but that was their tough luck!

My first Sunday at church after this enforced layoff was a nightmare. I celebrated the Eucharist and did all that I was supposed to, but I felt like an utter hypocrite. My assistant preached. It was a challenging sermon, but I found it impossible to concentrate my mental energies enough to listen to his words. When we reached the place in the service where the congregation joins in reciting the Creed I almost threw up.

"We believe . . . ," I began.

The congregation joined me, ". . . in one God, the Father, the Almighty, Maker of heaven and earth, and of all that is seen and unseen. . . ."

I was okay so far. The words were familiar, but despite the struggle I was having with my beliefs, I reckoned I could recite the Nicene formula without allowing it to have an impact on my mind. But as we proceeded I found myself straining to keep going. Nausea began rising from the pit of my stomach.

"We believe in one Lord, Jesus Christ, the only Son of God, eternally begotten of the Father, God from God, Light from Light, true God from true God, begotten not made, of one Being with the Father. . . ."

With many years of theological study under my belt, I had a far better idea of the intricacies of these words than anyone else in the building. Did I really believe these concepts in which I was leading the congregation? I couldn't say that I did, but then I wasn't sure that I didn't. The nausea continued to rise. I wanted to run from the sanctuary and vomit, but I kept going. By now sweat was dripping in great beads from my brow.

". . . For our sake he was crucified under Pontius Pilate; he suffered death and was buried. On the third day he rose again according to the Scriptures; he ascended into heaven. . . ."

The Resurrection and Ascension. What could my tortured mind make of these great doctrines? Were they facts or wishful fantasies conjured up by the first followers of Jesus? If they were the latter, then all who walked in their footsteps were victims of the biggest con job in history. Had I really given my best years to propagating the cover-up story of an obscure first-century rabbi suffering from megalomania?

The first occasion on which I had worried over the intellectual consistency of the Christian faith was during my senior year in high school. Strangely enough, I was going over the same ground again. As a man entering middle age, with college and seminary education behind me, I was in a better position to argue the subtleties with myself. But the big questions were still, "Who is this Jesus?" and "Did he really rise from the dead?"

"We believe in the Holy Spirit, the Lord, the giver of life, who proceeds from the Father and the Son. . . ."

The "Filioque Clause." I thought, "Did the Eastern and Western churches actually excommunicate one another in the eleventh century over this apparently harmless formula?"

For half the people in the church, the words were innocuous, coming forth easily yet having only a limited impact on their minds. But their priest was fighting a battle to the death inside himself, wondering where the streams of life would take him if he let go of the meaning behind these apparently harmless formularies.

And the Holy Spirit. His task was to convict of sin. Was I being convicted of sin? Although I had done an awful lot of confessing in the preceding months, was he still convicting me or was I convicting myself? Was he telling me to get out of the ministry for the sake of my own health and that of the Christian community?

". . . We look for the resurrection of the dead, and the life of the world to come. Amen."

"Thank God, it's over," I thought. I was swimming in a sea of sweat and feeling dreadful. But the nightmare was far from over. I still had to lead the congregation in the confession of sin. And when we had all addressed our petition for forgiveness to the Lord, I then had to stand before the people and, in the name of God, pronounce absolution. Who was I that I should speak these words? I felt like throwing myself prostrate before the altar and proclaiming in a loud voice that I was the greatest of sinners—"the chief of sinners," as the apostle Paul put it.

By the end of the service I was a wreck. I had dreaded the thought of consecrating the bread and wine in the great Eucharist prayer and had wondered if I could manage it without becoming completely unhinged. To my surprise, leading this part of the worship had not been as bad as I had expected. It was hardly fun, but to prepare myself before the service I had reread the twenty-sixth of the Thirty-Nine Articles of Religion: "Of the unworthiness of the Ministers, which hinders not the effect of the Sacraments."

I found solace in the words the Reformers had written: "Neither is the effect of Christ's ordinance taken away by their wickedness, nor the grace of God's gifts diminished from such . . . because of Christ's institution and promise, although they be ministered by evil men."

In my own eyes I was an evil man all right, but at least I clung to the consolation that my actions would only do limited damage to the faith of the congregation that had called me to be its rector some years earlier. When the organ postlude was being played and I was shaking hands at the door, I knew my pastoral ministry was nearly over. The only thing left was to work out a schedule for an orderly departure from the parish.

Many expressed their pleasure at having me up front again and, hoping to buoy me up, told me how well I looked. These words just poured salt into the wounds of my soul. At that moment I felt physically dreadful and spiritually worse. After greeting people at the door, the next ordeal was that hallowed element of American church life, the coffee hour.

Rachel was sitting by a window with a cluster of friends. She looked wistfully in my direction, but I grabbed my coffee and became part of a group of men discussing the prospects of the high school basketball team as the season moved toward its climax. Basketball has never been high on my agenda, but it was better than the hangdog misery of my wife.

Mary Ellen came along and separated me from the group.

"Thanks for stepping in—basketball's not my baby," I tried to say in a jaunty manner. I have always been pretty good at acting.

There was little room on Mary Ellen's agenda for small talk. She got straight to the point. "What's going on between you and Rachel?"

Covered with confusion, I stammered, "What do you mean?"

"You know damned well what I mean, Jeremy Wilkinson. I watched you walk in just now. You ignored her and joined a bunch of guys whose interests are diametrically opposed to your own. I've been watching you for a number of years now, and it doesn't take a sleuth to know when a marriage is struggling. Yours is, isn't it?"

Looking down at my shoes, I nodded.

"And I'd bet my bottom dollar that you are crucifying one another with words. I'd be surprised if there is any physical violence between you."

"Right again," I muttered.

"And now you are thinking 'when will this interfering old busybody get off my case?'"

"Something like that," was all I could reply. Trying to improve things, I continued, "But you are hardly old."

The statement was true, but soft soap had little impact on such a person as this. A graying woman with a less than perfect marriage of her own, Mary Ellen knew more than most about life's troubles. She was a brusque lady with a short fuse who had managed to support her son and daughter through their growing years until they had successful careers and happy homes of their own. With them off her hands, she was always looking for lame ducks to nurture. From where I was sitting, it appeared that Rachel and I were the candidates upon whom the lot had fallen.

101

A gentleness came into her eyes. "I'll be around if ever you want a shoulder to cry on. But remember this, I'll have Rachel crying on the other one. I'm darned if I will allow a relationship like yours to come to pieces."

With this parting shot she left the hall, and I scurried back to my office to ponder where I was to go from here. How much longer could I stay with Rachel? How much longer could a priest with so shaky a faith as mine continue as rector of the parish? How many people were aware of the dreadful misery through which our family was passing? The list of questions grew, and I had no way of answering them. My gut was tense, and the tears began to flow.

10

The worst part of my departure from St. Mary's was the reception following my final service. I wished I could have followed the choir out that morning and just kept on walking, but for the sake of both the congregation and myself, I had to make as good a conclusion to my pastorate as possible.

I saw tears in the eyes of some and detected muted anger in the jaws of others. One group was genuinely relieved to see me go. Others were hurt that I should depart in such a broken state. Had I been leaving nobly, on my way to another position in ministry, there would have been a positive atmosphere at the farewell. But such was not the case.

Few of the people seemed to understand the crisis our family was experiencing, and those who did were bewildered. I had preached a poor sermon, but most seemed satisfied that I had done my best. In the highly charged emotional atmosphere, I sensed that even a few seemed moved and warmed by my words.

There were a few speeches, hands were shaken, coffee and cookies were consumed, but it was obvious that folk did not want to drag the suffering out any longer than necessary. Soon the crowds were going. By lunchtime I was left alone to wallow in my misery. I have never set eyes on many of those people again. They include some wonderful people whom I genuinely miss. But, quite honestly, it has been a relief to extricate myself from the lives of others.

Not everyone was happy to see me go. Just the other day, several years after this crisis, I received a note from a former member of St. Mary's who has retired and moved to sunnier climes. She wrote,

> Jeremy, Ellis and I feel the people at the church gave you a raw deal when you were there. Leadership like yours comes once in a lifetime for a congregation like ours, and we are sorry that the "ruling clique" was unable to see the gifts you brought into our midst.
>
> There is no way that we can make amends for the harm that was done to you and your family, but from the bottom of our hearts we thank you for the blessing you were to us during your time at St. Mary's. If you are ever in the Fort Myers area, you know that you, Rachel, and the children will always have a bed for the night. . . .

I have had several letters like this. Such tokens of appreciation have done much to lay to rest ghosts from the past and mitigate the pain we suffered at the time. Eleanor's comments may be an exaggeration, but they come from a warm heart. Of all the people in that congregation, she more than most learned how unrealistic are the demands that are sometimes placed on an American pastor in the latter part of the twentieth century.

When we got home from the church, the family sat down together for lunch. In the midst of this somber meal Rachel and I immediately indulged in a flaming row. She ran into the living room wailing her head off, and I marched upstairs, packed a bag, and went to Alice's.

So began an off-again–on-again relationship with my wife. For weeks I felt like a human yo-yo—sleeping at home one night but hot-footing it off to Alice's for days, or even a week, when the going got tough. Then I would be home perhaps for a few hours before something happened that would provoke me to walk out again.

Having heard how badly Rachel and I were doing, Rebecca got in touch. We met and talked. I was certain that my thing—whatever one could call it—with Rebecca was over. And I told her so. I had moved on, and so had she. Now that she did not have to pretend to be dependent on a man, she was learning to make a life of her own; but as she did, her values were changing. I didn't like what I saw. It was clear that when the chips were down, we each had a different way of reacting. I got crushed. She adapted.

I still found her an extraordinarily attractive woman, but in my distress I knew it would not be helpful to any of us if she were a further complicating factor in the issues with which Rachel and I were wrestling. We promised to keep in touch. In my loneliness I did cry on her shoulder once or twice, but as the weeks passed, the calls grew less frequent until they eventually stopped.

Part of the reason for my lack of interest was that my self-esteem had reached rock bottom. I had little respect for myself and I could not believe that anyone else would even want to give me the time of day.

"What person in their right mind would want to be involved in any way with a dropout like me?" I would ask myself over and over again.

*   *   *

Terms for my severance from the church were dictated by the bishop. If he had not stepped in on my behalf, I do not know what would have happened. I do not think the leaders of the parish wanted to be mean, but I had the impression that they felt it necessary to rap me across the knuckles for failing them. I might have responded similarly if I had been in their position.

They gave me six months sabbatical and allowed my family to live in the rectory until we were able to find another place. They also paid hospitalization and so forth through that period. This gave me time to begin to get back on my feet.

But such safety nets are not always provided. I have met pastors who burned out and then have been shown the door without a trace of generosity. Many of them were turned into derelict creatures who were literally robbed of everything. Some have continued down the slope into spiritual, emotional, and material poverty. The question continually arises, "Why is it that the Christian church is the only organization on earth that shoots its wounded?"

I wish there were a reasonable answer to that question. Forgiveness and mercy are at the heart of the gospel, but many church people have yet to discover how they might demonstrate these virtues with their pastors.

Indeed, the bishop's safety net gave me time and space to get my head back together. But I had been stripped of *everything*. Being jobless felt like being castrated. For the first time in my adult life I was without ministry, without employment, and virtually without family. Although I still saw my wife and kids occasionally, it had become a bizarre and inadequate relationship.

Former parishioners avoided or spurned me if they met me in public. One evening, when staying with Alice, I went to one of those ear-shattering concerts at my children's school. In front of me sat a family from St. Mary's. Ron, the husband, was embarrassed but attempted to make polite conversation, talking about the expansion of his business. Linda would have nothing to do with me. She pursed her lips whenever she turned in my direction; and if looks could kill. . . .

She had been one of those people who had idolized the rector, believing that every "man of God" walked six inches off the ground and had a hotline to heaven: but woe betide if I let her down. Now I had done just that, and she could not find it in her heart to forgive me. After depositing son and trumpet on my wife's doorstep, I drove back to Alice's wondering what I would have done had I been in Linda's position. Sadly, I concluded that I probably would have behaved as she had.

In order to keep away from people, I transferred my account to a branch miles from anywhere St. Mary's people might bank and started taking my clothes to a dry cleaners in another suburb. When I went food shopping I would go to a supermarket that I knew was hardly ever patronized by

106

members of the parish. That it was in a rougher section made no difference; at least I was anonymous.

So here I was—a nobody living a limbo-like existence and terrified that the money would run out and I might still be without work. I sprayed resumes all over Boston like bullets from a machine gun. I relentlessly pursued leads that came up on my network. As I had discovered before resigning, no one seemed particularly interested in a washed-up priest. That I was no longer an active minister probably made matters even more difficult.

How do you answer the question, "Mr. Wilkinson, why do you want to leave the ministry?" I found that however I tried to answer, it was a black mark against me. I hope I am not arrogant in noting that many of those who interviewed me were people of limited talents. My resume may have suggested that if I were to join their organization, I had the ability to challenge their security or chances of promotion once I had learned the ropes.

Then there were the weekends. Weekends were such a novelty that at first I wasn't at all sure I knew how to use them. I would roam about the house trying not to get in Rachel's way or disappear to Alice's where my wife would not disturb me.

One bleak winter afternoon I was sitting in Alice's living room watching something on the television with her. I don't recall the program, but something was said that resonated with my own pain, and I came completely undone. For an hour or more I wept like a baby. I had not cried such bitter and uninhibited tears for many years. They burned my cheeks, made my throat sore, and drained all the energy from me. Every now and then Alice would put a motherly arm around my shoulders. I would shake it off. Instinctively I knew this was one battle I had to fight alone.

So began an extended period when I would have to hide myself away every day and weep. When I was at Alice's I would cry myself to sleep, at home I would lock myself in the bathroom. My only consolation was that Rachel's tears were as intense and as bitter as my own. When at home, I would often lie in the guest room in the middle of the night listening to her sobs echoing down the heating ducts.

We struggled with one another in counseling, trying to work out how we were to relate in the future. I did not want to lose her, yet at the same time I could not imagine living with her for the rest of my earthly pilgrimage. She had her friends bolstering her at the same time as mine commiserated with me.

As the advice poured in from all quarters, we were told to get ourselves good lawyers. I balked at the thought of an attorney raking over the embers of our marriage and breaking up our household. Rachel did not like the idea any better.

Instead of a lawyer, we tried a divorce mediator. He was helpful, but it turned out that neither of us had the will to go through with his process either. We both loved our children and were anxious for their well-being. My involvement with them was belated, but my paternal concern was genuine. I loved my children and wanted to be their nonabsent father. Also, our religious conditioning did not allow us to regard divorce as a serious option.

Rachel and I are both as stubborn as mules. With the devil of divorce staring us in the eyes, neither of us was willing to admit to defeat. So on we struggled, trying to make a silk purse from a sow's ear.

Our misery was total, yet Rachel seemed to be coping far better than I. Because I was away from her so much and watched her from a distance, I found myself becoming a grudging admirer of her indomitable spirit. She found herself a job, went off each morning, did a good day's work, and then came home and cared for the kids. All I could do was run round in a frenzy looking for a new career but getting nowhere.

What I failed to realize was that counseling was beginning to pay off. The demolition process had finally over and rebuilding had started. In a peculiarly painful session Jonathan asked Rachel and me to talk about our respective childhoods. As I listened to her, I was brought face-to-face with aspects of her personality that were a revelation to me.

Then I told my story. As I spoke, I too uncovered uncut diamonds in my past—truths about myself and my upbringing that made sense of the position I now found myself in. After that session, instead of going off in opposite directions, Rachel and I had coffee together. It was the first time in months that we had been out alone together. I cannot remember when we had previously had such a satisfying conversation.

When she left the little restaurant to get home to the children, I was sorry to see her go. I needed several more cups of coffee to ponder the experience. Was Rachel gaining new poise and dignity, or was I seeing her through different eyes?

Dusk was descending, and from my window seat in that little Italian cafe, I watched the crowds hurrying home. Unconsciously I was comparing the women on the sidewalk with my wife. Many of them were obviously more glamorous—even under layers of winter clothing—but they seemed to lack the depth of the girl I had met when I was a student so long ago.

I was staying with Alice at that time and started to wonder whether I should go back home. On following days Rachel and I had several more revealing conversations and even went for a walk together. It looked as if all the pieces were coming together again when suddenly something trivial and stupid had us fighting like cat and dog. I retired to my corner, she to hers, and it seemed like we were back where we started.

In retrospect, I cannot understand how our emotions survived the stretching and snapping. Rachel could be the most aggravating woman in New England, perhaps even in the whole United States. I would fume and ferment over her attitudes and behavior. Over dinner I would give the long-suffering Alice an earful of my feelings, and she would patiently listen as I vented my wrath.

Then she would say, with a twinkle in her eye, "Now, Jeremy, be a good man and help me with the dishes."

Alice was very clever at being down-to-earth, and in my state of heightened anxiety, that was extremely helpful, for I was having trouble handling the practicalities of life. Only since then have I discovered how shrewd her perceptions were of the healing process that was gradually drawing husband and wife together again.

*   *   *

I have never entered St. Mary's Church since the day I quit as rector. On the Sundays following my resignation I visited in the back pew of other Episcopal churches, eventually settling to hang my hat at Trinity Church, Copley Square, in the shadow of the John Hancock Building. In so large a congregation I could worship in anonymity each Sunday.

While the pieces of my faith were still fragmented, without the pressure of congregational life, I was in a position to reconstruct a framework of belief. Now that I did not have to be in church every Sunday morning, it was dawning on me that I wanted to go. There is an element of perverseness in my character that has a habit of rearing its ugly head every now and again.

Rachel continued at St. Mary's, being feted as the hard-done-by, misused wife by my antagonists. I persuaded myself to think she was enjoying the limelight but discovered later that she was hating it and was herself looking for a graceful way out of the parish.

I would sit in Trinity Church in a state of paranoia, wondering what was being said this week, thinking the people at St. Mary's had ganged up with my wife against me. Parishes have an ability to take on a corporate identity and, like a seductress, separate a pastor from his wife. The people out there in the suburbs had played that game on our marriage; now it seemed that they were going in for the kill.

Some of the anger that erupted in our fierce battles at that stage in the proceedings centered around life at St. Mary's. I don't know what I wanted, but I longed for my family to be free of those ties that bound us, even loosely, to the people there.

110

Then something rather extraordinary and unexpected happened. It gave Rachel the excuse to leave St. Mary's, and it put us both on the same side of a tug-of-war.

I had rented a post office box for my mail. One dreary evening as I returned from a fruitless day of job hunting, I dropped by to pick it up. All that was there was a note from the treasurer of the parish. Ben Schroeder was a mild-mannered man. He had been a civil servant his whole life and did a wonderful job of keeping the books of the parish and ensuring that funds were accounted for down to the very last penny.

I was not expecting what fell from the envelope. As I read it there in the lobby of the post office, I swore under my breath and then uttered an insult aloud. A couple of old gentlemen, who looked as if they had been sheltering there all afternoon from the wind, and their wives turned toward me in astonishment. For a moment their reworking of the Social Security system could wait. Why would a total stranger make such an exhibition of himself?

Storming out of the post office, I jumped into my car and sped to the rectory, where Rachel was just getting the evening meal.

"Come home for dinner, Jeremy?" she asked with a forced cheeriness.

"No, darn it. Leave that confounded pot of spaghetti alone and tell me the meaning of this."

I thrust Ben's note under her nose.

Wiping her hands on her apron, she took the already crumpled piece of paper from my hand. She read it through once, looked up at me, reread it, and then went off like a firecracker.

"Who do those people think they are? What are they playing at? I can assure you this is the first I have heard of this."

She took the letter and read it aloud, her voice tinged with sarcasm:

111

Dear Mr. Wilkinson, ["Good heavens, Jeremy! You've been away *so* long they can no longer remember your first name."]

This is to inform you that at a meeting of the vestry on Monday evening last, it was agreed to allow your family to remain in the rectory for a few months until you have made other suitable arrangements.

While accepting the bishop's overgenerous terms of severance ["They were only what you were due"], we feel it is only fair that you reimburse us a fair market rental for the use of this prime piece of real estate. Therefore, on the first of next month, we expect to receive from you a check for $600 to cover rental, and of course, we are assuming that you will handle the cost of the utilities.

On behalf of the vestry of St. Mary's Episcopal Church, I remain yours sincerely,

A. Benjamin Schroeder

"Ben Schroeder would never have the nerve to write a letter like this," Rachel concluded. "I smell less savory characters behind this."

She was white with anger at this point. I could remember that when I was a child, my father would get so livid with my sister after some tasteless prank that he turned white with rage. But I had never seen this side of Rachel before.

She was magnificent. She ranted and raved as she marched up and down the kitchen waving a spaghetti ladle. She kept going while the children came down to eat. She was still fuming as she stacked the dirty plates and silverware in the dishwasher.

For once, I could not get a word in edgewise. And for the first time in many a weary month, we found ourselves wholeheartedly on the same side of a dispute. Dropping with fatigue, Rachel eventually slumped inelegantly into the arms of her favorite overstuffed chair.

Her hair was all over the place, a streak of spaghetti sauce was smeared on her right cheek, and her face was a blotchy patchwork of sweat and the remainder of the day's make-up. As I looked at the woman half-sitting, half-lying there wearing a dirty apron and no shoes and sporting a huge run in her hose, I knew that I loved her and was only half a man without her.

Leaning over, I kissed her on the forehead. She turned her head up and gave me a faint smile of pleasure. If the children had not been racing all over the place, it is highly likely that we would have ended up in bed together.

Later that night I drove back to Alice's where I had been staying for the past week, wondering how Rachel and I could get it back together. Somehow a line had been crossed. I knew it, and I was confident from that look Rachel had given me that she did too. Whatever it took by way of counseling, talking through the hard things, and saving each other a little pride, I felt that we would make it. I knew now that we both really wanted to.

11

The story I am telling is actually many stories. It is one about the pressures of pastoral ministry. It is one about the set of symptoms that accompanies the experience of burnout. It is also one about a person's battle with doubt and unbelief. When menacing (faith) problems of any kind impose themselves on a layperson, he or she has the liberty to slip into the background of church life while sorting out these vital issues.

The layperson is not expected to lead worship, preach, comfort the sick and dying, or teach the young about Jesus in season and out of season. Whether it is right or wrong, this is what congregations pay their pastor for. If his spirituality develops a disorder or his Christian commitment starts coming unthreaded, he is often expected to carry on as if nothing were wrong. Few churches realize their minister is as prone to ailments of the soul as anyone else, if not more so.

In all my years prior to this crisis, my experience of spiritual disfunction was the occasional insignificant doubt nibbling at the fringes of my soul. By contrast, burnout was a sinkhole that swallowed my faith whole. Perhaps the most frightening moment of my life was when I stammered out, "I'm not really sure that I believe in God anymore."

Accompanying that confession of unbelief went the dreams and aspirations I had cherished since my adult life began. The doubt came on gradually, flashing warnings. I felt an increasing dis-ease with the Good News of Jesus Christ, but by the time I got around to doing something about the

115

unstable ground beneath my spiritual feet, the process of erosion had gone too far.

With startling rapidity, I slid from a place where I was struggling to hold onto beliefs I had held dear to one where I tried to convince myself that I didn't care too much whether God currently existed or ever had. That I really was concerned was part of the game I played with myself. But I had reached a point where something in my conscious mind was persuading me that I had spent too many years pursuing a fool's errand.

My devotional life withered on the vine, and my preaching became a charade. I knew it was vital for me to get out of ministry, to go back to basics and think the faith through again. A wiser person would have made his malaise clear to the lay leadership of his congregation, but not I. I hinted that everything was far from right, hoping that they would pick up my distress signals and offer me the time and space I needed.

They didn't. It was unrealistic of me to expect them to: I should have been more direct and asked for what I needed.

Jonathan picked up the faith dimension of my crisis immediately. In one of our first sessions he asked, "Jeremy, how's your spiritual discipline?"

"Virtually nonexistent."

"Hummm." Billows of smoke rose from his freshly lit pipe. "What do you mean by that?"

"Well, I suppose I'm not surprised," he said.

I waited for the counselor to go on. There was silence. Then at a slow and measured pace, he spelled out the close relationship between emotional exhaustion and spiritual ill-health. This was not news to me, but it was good to be reminded.

"What are you having problems with?" he then questioned.

"Just about everything."

"Be more specific," he said, encouraging me along.

So I spilled the beans. My prayer life had reached a dead end; apart from preparation for sermons and talks, I seldom picked up the Bible. When I did read it, it seemed about as

116

relevant to me as the mutterings of some primitive shaman. These initial symptoms of spiritual distress were giving way to something more ominous. Now I was finding myself wondering about the nature, even the existence, of the Almighty himself.

"You're not the first to travel this route, you know. This is a 'dark night of the soul'; this is the apparent withdrawal of God. When you come out of the blackness of the tunnel into which you have been plunged, your faith will be richer and stronger."

"Thanks a million, pal," I gushed, trying to be jocular. "A lot of good pie-in-the-sky-when-I-die is doing me right now."

"There's more comfort in my words than you are prepared to recognize at this stage of the game," came the rejoinder.

"But what have I done to make this all happen?" I queried.

"First of all, when did you last do something to look after your own emotional health?" The question was meant to be rhetorical. I said nothing. After a moment's silence, while he tamped down the tobacco in his pipe, he continued.

"From what you have said, you have had a lengthening shopping list of doubts and faith problems tucked away at the back of your mind, but you haven't done anything about it. I expect you hoped things would eventually straighten themselves out."

He was about to continue when I blurted out, "They always have in the past!"

He looked up and smiled gently. "Not this time, though. You've been brushing them under the rug, and now the accumulation of difficulties is tripping you up whenever you walk past that spot. Right?"

"Something like that," I replied sheepishly.

By the time I tried to walk away from life in Boston and head for the West Coast, God had become little more than an abstract idea. Deep within me there was something that longed to throw itself before him in prostrate adoration. If only I could be sure that he existed.

Attempting to run away was my admission of defeat. In

utter despair Job's wife had told him to be done with God. My bungled retreat from the scene of battle was probably my way of attempting to follow her instructions. I had tried every way I knew of to get a response from God, and they hadn't worked. Now I would have a go at shocking him. And if I couldn't get through to him that way, then I didn't know what I would do.

I don't recommend this approach. Nevertheless, it proved to be a turning point. Once I reached the bottom, I was ready for the long road back. Many months were to pass before my spiritual health returned to anything like normal, but within weeks God once more became a reality for me, even if a distant one. I cannot precisely tell why. There were no trumpets, just the slow, quiet realization that I had been barking up the wrong tree.

There grew within me the conviction that however bad circumstances got, "The Lord of Hosts is with us, the God of Jacob is our refuge." Some days these words from Psalm 46 would be the only devotions I could muster, but muster them I did, and they carried me through the storms. This short verse of Scripture marked the rebirth of my desire to have a relationship with the Almighty.

My slide into doubt and unbelief was marked by an overpowering sense of guilt. I had good reason to feel guilty: I was not doing my job properly. I had toyed with a relationship that played a part in all but destroying my marriage, and I had tried to walk away from the solemn vows I had made on the day that I was ordained. Trying to run away was an attempt to escape my sense of guilt rather than face up to it.

But then, like all conscientious people, I allowed my psyche to amplify those guilt feelings. As they nagged away at me, they started to expand. With ever-growing speed these unhealthy tentacles of distress poked their way into every facet of life, wreaking havoc.

As the reality of God started reasserting itself, so did the desire to make confession. Sessions with Jonathan became protracted periods of breast-beating as I shone the light of day on sins both real and imagined. Just as I had exaggerated the extent of deliberate evil, so now I exaggerated the need to make amends. I wanted to be clean, but most of all I wanted to *feel* clean. I yearned to be free of the sea of sin that I imagined had swept over me.

It took months for this sense of worthlessness to moderate. In my own eyes I was a worm. God had shown grace, mercy, and generosity toward me in the past, but I had ratted on him. I am pretty certain that I did not think I had done the unforgivable, but I had a notion that I had come close to it.

Perhaps I had "cherished" the idea for many years that the Almighty was a supernatural tyrant who took delight in hurting his erring children. Perhaps I had a hidden motivation for Christian service: to keep the wrath of a vengeful God at arm's length. Now this misconception had to be purged. I slowly came to realize that although I loved Jesus, the Good Shepherd, with all my heart, at the back of my mind I had the idea that all I had to do was make one false move and he would whack this erring sheep across the backside with his staff!

I would spend hours lying on the sofa staring at the ceiling or walking the beach, untangling the knots that I had tied round my mind and soul. It was a voyage of discovery: I was not only uncovering facets of Jeremy Wilkinson that I had not previously encountered, but I was on a journey of exploration into the very heart of God.

Little by little Jesus came back into focus, and as he did, I saw him in ways I had never been able to before. There was a love, graciousness, and tolerance about this dying Savior that was new to me. Why hadn't I seen it before? Previously, I had been conscious of his power and glory, but now I was seeing the long-suffering Lord into whose eyes the angry man who was to become the apostle Paul, stared on the Damascus Road.

As I started reading the Bible again, it was to the apostle Paul's autobiographical passages that I turned. Did he *really* consider himself "the chief of sinners"? If he did, then I knew exactly how he felt, for that is how I perceived myself. He had persecuted the church, and by my shortcomings I had let it down—there was little difference between us.

This rediscovery of grace did not come with a great rush. It nuzzled up against me with the gentleness of a kitten asking for attention; as I gave the attention it yearned for, it rewarded me a thousandfold. The experience was not unlike C. S. Lewis being "surprised by joy."

About a year after the crisis I found myself writing these words to a friend:

> Until I went through this horrendous experience, I must have spent many hours in the pulpit waxing eloquent about the grace of God. My words probably sounded hollow because I am not sure that I had started to understand the magnitude of God's love. Now I think I do.

> The effect that this understanding has had upon me is nothing short of revolutionary. God is infinitely more glorious than I ever imagined! In light of this experience, I have become more tolerant, not just of failures in myself, but also in other people. The love that has been showered upon me I am able to share with others.

Although many months have passed since I wrote those words, I realize that I cannot fully live by them. I guess I am a kind of "backslider." There are times when an overwhelming sense of guilt overpowers me. Occasionally I find myself crumpling up inside, and in my imagination I am transported back to those difficult days. Then I start thinking, "Did I really do that or say those things? I must have been out of my mind. How is it that God can ever begin to forgive me and entrust new ministries to me?"

My ponderings illustrate how typical I am of so many clergy. We find it difficult to tolerate our own frailties when we might be quite generous about the shortcomings of others. Perhaps we start out thinking we are inoculated against the power of sin as a result of our ordination. The result is that when we finally stumble, we lay illogical, distorted, and masochistic guilt trips on ourselves.

Not long ago I found myself sitting beside a Baptist pastor

on a plane. It was a long flight, and our conversation quickly progressed beyond polite formalities. We shared in depth our lives and experience of ministry. Having told him my story, I concluded with the throwaway line, "I'm not sure that I will ever be really able to forgive myself."

"Perhaps," came my new friend's reply, "but whether you like it or not, you *are* forgiven."

When counseling others, I have lost count of the number of times that I have said something similar. Perhaps it was appropriate that these words were thrown back at me by another minister. I had never seen him before, and I have never seen him since. Come to think of it, I'm not sure he even told me his name! But his words have encouraged me to apply the love of the Cross to my struggle to forgive myself for failing to live up to my own high standards during a time of considerable personal stress.

Had my odyssey not taken me through this grinding experience, I am not sure that I would have fully grasped the yearning that so many have to feel forgiven.

I made a commitment to Christ in my teenage years and could talk a good line about the grace of God. Only now was this youthful commitment coming of age. At last I could empathize with the businessman who hates himself because he compromised his standards in a recent deal or with the suburban homemaker who, at the age of forty-three, has fallen out of love with her husband and yearns for an apartment, independence, and "a life of her own."

My bubble of self-righteousness had been burst. When I found myself tempted to condemn folks who, in my opinion, did not measure up, the little voice of my conscience would whisper, "Have you forgotten so quickly?"

While I knew that the Christian gospel was about forgiveness, I had spent a great deal of time standing in judgment over men and women who were dying for words of comfort. While my words might have spoken of a God of love, my actions and body language would suggest that he had a vindictive side to his personality.

What has been interesting since my own ordeal by fire is

that men and women whose conduct leaves something to be desired have been much more ready to open up the deepest recesses of their lives to me. Maybe they sense that something significant has happened to me and expect that I may have a better understanding of what they are going through and that I will be able to speak God's words of comfort and encouragement to them.

Yet how quickly I find myself playing the condemnation game again. How difficult it is to break the lifelong habit of blaming personal and global ills on someone else. My temptation is to project my hobgoblins onto everyone else rather than take responsibility for the part I have played in a mess that is waiting to be cleared up. How eager I am to underestimate the power of the One who hung there on Good Friday taking the world's woes on his shoulders.

During the protracted period of counseling with Jonathan, we were not merely working on the destructive forces that I had unleashed on my own life and therefore on the lives of all those around me; we were also attempting to grasp the theological dimension of my struggle and the spiritual implications of all that I had been through.

Once the initial logjam was broken, again and again I would attempt to take the weight of my sins upon my own shoulders. Instead of blaming my hobgoblins on others, now I wanted them all to myself.

"Why can't you let them go?" Jonathan had asked one day in exasperation.

"I don't know," I murmured in reply. "I honestly don't know."

"I'm not sure you really want to," he fired back at me. "I think you enjoy wallowing in your own misery. There is something habitual about the way in which you flagellate yourself."

We worked around these issues for many hours. Although I did not reach any conclusions, an emotional balance gradually started to return, so I began to gain a new perspective on things that before had been a closed book.

The long road back to spiritual health had any number of

landmarks. It was a journey marked by unexpected twists and turns. In the obscurity of the back pew of another congregation I was in a position either to doubt or to dissect any and every aspect of the Christian gospel.

During the time that my own emotional storms were subsiding, I would round an unexpected corner and stumble over treasures that added new richness to the life of faith. Most of the time I would regard such events as serendipitous. Now I know there was more happening than chance revelations.

Unbeknown to me, literally hundreds of people across the nation and even overseas were praying for me and my family. While friends and colleagues in Boston were close at hand giving their support, others were helping us forward in the only way they could—on their knees. From this perspective in time, I am convinced that these people played a significant role in my recovery.

Nine months after the crisis broke, I knelt before my bishop. In his presence, and surrounded by close family and friends, I renewed my ordination vows. On the day that I had first made those promises, they had seemed very academic. Now, as I made them again, they were charged with fresh meaning and overpowering significance. Tears welled up in me as the bishop placed his hands on my head and recommissioned me for ministry in the universal church.

12

I started writing my experiences down soon after I quit as rector of St. Mary's, when the pain was still fresh to my memory. The work has proceeded spasmodically over several years since then. My life today is very different from my life through those dreadful days of deep crisis. I can see now what I could not see then because I have a firm place to stand. Before, I was face-down and confused, disoriented, lost.

Telling the story has sometimes been an uncomfortable business because I have been forced to relive the past, a past that I would gladly put behind me and forget. There are occasions when I have had to abandon the project in order to step back and recover my equilibrium. This chapter comes after one such long hiatus.

I have been asking myself why I delayed so long. The excuses come tumbling readily off my pen: I've been too busy. . . . I want to obliterate the past and get on with the new opportunities life offers. . . . I ignored my children dreadfully for many years; in my attempts to rectify that situation I have to spend more time with them.

All these answers are true, but none reaches the root of the matter. Perhaps the real reason for my unwillingness to continue the story is that I do not know how it will end. Each day I live with the positive and negative consequences of those months of agony. As I said when I began, this is a story without a conclusion—but there ought be a place to draw the line.

That I am a different person than the one who underwent

the experience of burnout is without question. I am a wiser and, in a way, a sadder man. For many years I retained an element of naïveté, a residual childishness, that has now gone forever.

Recently, I was visiting a city on the other side of the country. Sunday morning found me part of the congregation of a well-known church. The preacher at that service spoke about the various "baptisms" of our life, one being the inevitable "loss of innocence." I am inclined to think that when I burned out something like that happened to me.

I was not only brought face-to-face with the darkness that hovers on the perimeter of all our lives, but also forced to examine the shadow side of my own personality—the darkness within that would encroach and destroy if given the opportunity. During that "dark night of the soul" I was apparently unable or unwilling to respond creatively to the loving-kindness of my God.

I find myself wrestling with the questions that surround this phenomenon. Did I experience such Godforsakenness because *I* turned my back on the pleadings of the Almighty, or was it because *he* seemed to withdraw beyond the reach of my most fervent prayers? I am distressed by the willfulness of some of my actions. But had I been conscious that underneath were the everlasting arms, would I have continued along the downhill path to self-destruction?

A further question I struggle with is how much was this bound to happen? Here I was—a capable person frustrated in my ministry, my career, and my marriage. I was reaching the midpoint in life when any man worth his salt is going to do a lot of rethinking and reassessing. Is it fatalistic to expect that a series of events would occur that would precipitate such a crisis?

For me this living nightmare was a process through which I passed; others have not been so fortunate. During the last few years I have come across many people, ordained and lay, whose permanently damaged lives are testimony to the power of burnout and a difficult midlife transition.

The shelves of my library are packed with works of

biography. I have found myself returning to this collection of life stories, searching for a different set of facts than those of my own past. Previously I had concentrated on what these persons managed to achieve. More recently I have been attempting to discover what they were like—as persons. Perhaps that is a natural consequence of reaching middle age.

My preliminary findings are that many individuals have experienced spiritual and psychological stagnation at this point in their lives, have tumbled into an abyss somewhere inside themselves, but emerge from the crisis with a poise and stability that did not previously exist. Martin Luther is a supreme example of this phenomenon. When he later mused upon the experience, he wrote, "I did not learn my theology all at once, but I had to search deeper for it, where my temptations took me."

What I find most depressing is the number who seem to lose their identity in the melting pot of advancing middle age. There are too many washed-up former ministers across the length and breadth of this great land. It would appear that either something within them or the circumstances in which they wrestled their dragons overpowered them. Maybe the theological education that prepared them for ministry filled them with concepts but did not provide the resources for them to search deeper, where their temptations take them.

My Presbyterian minister-friend, Kenneth, disappeared down that crevasse. Occasionally I run across guys like him selling insurance or real estate, working in some kind of counseling or managing someone else's business. Some people are not "designed" to handle pastoral ministry all their lives, but the guys I have in mind wistfully long to return to ministry even though they know they cannot.

Many have gone off on a journey in search of mental and spiritual hygiene, but have become lost. They have looked in the wrong places for integrity of life and belief and have strayed down paths that have turned them into pariahs in the community that once gave shape and meaning to their lives. As I come into contact with such men, my heart goes out to them, and I wonder whether things might have been different if the church could have given them the space they needed.

Pondering my own past tends to make me morose. I am overwhelmed by guilt and start flagellating myself again. When I attempt to find answers to what are now imponderable questions, I wonder whether I am looking for excuses or am trying to do something that will somehow correct past errors. This, I am sure, results from that highly developed, almost neurotic, sense of personal responsibility that is the hallmark of many clergy.

Like everyone, I wish I could take credit for my own achievements and unload the responsibility for my shortcomings and failures upon someone or something else. I have done that as far back as I can remember and still toy with it occasionally. However, my commitment to Christian values urges me to be honest with myself. So I fall over backwards to take more than my fair share of responsibility for things that go awry. Perhaps it is impossible for any of us to be truly "balanced."

Sometimes during the worship service, as I prepare to preach, the blackness of the past floods in. I might remember something dreadful I said to Rachel or the forbidden sweetness of Rebecca's kisses. In so doing, the abyss comes up to meet me. I am overcome by a sense of unworthiness and feel incapable of mounting the pulpit steps to proclaim the Word of God to the people of God. On one such occasion, I seemed to be on the verge of physical paralysis.

I am haunted by the past. I cry out for the millionth time in confession, as if hoping to hear a voice from heaven that will speak to the nausea within me. My mind knows I am forgiven and renewed, yet personal insecurities keep me from accepting the fact.

All this can happen in a split second. Then I am reminded of Christ's body broken and blood poured out and remember that his grace is sufficient. This recollection enables me to take Bible and sermon notes in hand and, as a beggar who has been wonderfully fed, show other beggars where to find the food of eternal, abundant life.

I hope I will never forget that I am redeemed by God's grace alone. Although it is early yet, I believe that the constant reclaiming of this truth has added new depth and new humility to my life and to the ministry into which the Lord God Almighty has called me.

One of the tragedies of the modern church is that so many who experience burnout, instead of finding it a stepping-stone to a fresh realization of grace, discover it to be the cause of their downfall. Sometimes a congregation seems unable or unwilling to forgive past mistakes. Or it may be that the pastor himself is unable to own up to and deal with the contribution he made to his own demise. Maybe that was Kenneth's problem.

A figure who encourages me is Moses. He brutally murdered the Egyptian when seeking to make meaning of his life. Then he fled. It seemed as if his career was finished; all that remained was to live out the residue of his days in obscurity. So he buried himself on "the backside of the wilderness"; but God had other plans. The rebuilding process took a while, yet when it was through, Moses was a man whose inspired leadership would make him a pattern to millions over the millennia.

But Moses would not have been able to lead Israel out of slavery without that long spell of "lostness." In retrospect, I am not sure my theological education and spiritual formation helped me understand the importance of the wilderness in the process of maturation. If I had understood some of the necessary processes of spiritual growth, I might have made better use of this episode in my life.

In American churches, we say little about spiritual anguish and so leave Christians unprepared for the growing pains of faith. And clergy, part of whose calling is to walk through the vale of tears with believers, are not properly equipped to carry the burdens that are inevitably laid on them.

So many of the agonies and burdens my congregations shared with me, I internalized. Each Sunday morning I would look out across a sea of faces, many of whom were wrestling with problems that were grinding them into the ground, and I would feel the weight of their load crushing me. I knew the persons whose lives were teetering on the brink of disaster, and I earnestly desired to shepherd them past the precipices.

As they came and knelt at the Communion rail to receive the sacraments, I would pray for them individually as I handed them the sacramental bread and wine.

"The body of Christ keep you in eternal life," would be the words of my mouth, but in my heart I would continue, "and may these tokens of God's goodness strengthen you in your fight with depression, Mary."

About her husband I would pray, "And Tim, I know you are worried about your wife and job and the effect that so much time traveling is having on your teenage children. I notice they are not in church again today. God bless you and them."

I would pray over troubled marriages, terminal illnesses, struggles with alcoholism, financial worries, and career disappointments. I could pray this way because I knew their lives intimately. Often, unexpectedly, they would invite me to share their inmost thoughts. When they hurt, I hurt with them. My problem was that I helped them cope with their burdens by taking them on my own shoulders.

Often a parishioner would leave my office with a jaunty step, and I would collapse exhausted into my chair. They left feeling more at ease because they had shared the weight while I staggered around trying to find some way to cope with the consequence to myself of the confessions they might have made.

I believe the church is to be a hospital for sinners, but my deepening distress left me with the unanswered question, "Who cares for the doctor when he falls ill?" If the churches of our nation are to be pastored by healthy men and women, it is vital that we find ways of helping the clergy handle the contagious diseases of the soul.

On a bleak winter day, when there had been a fresh fall of snow and winter looked as if it would go on forever, Jonathan and I found ourselves talking about the way I coped with the burdens that people laid on me. He forced me to admit that I tended to lay them on my own shoulders.

By this time my theological orientation had returned sufficiently well for us to deal with the divine dimension of what had happened. So Jonathan said, "Now tell me what you believe about the cross of Christ."

It took us a while to unravel the implications of God becoming man, of our Lord's sinless life and sacrificial death. But in a fairly unsystematic way, we adventured into the heartland of our faith. Once we were there, Jonathan tossed out his "thought for the week": "You have learned and preached and taught others that at the foot of the cross we find redemption, right?"

I nodded.

"You recognize that if individuals and societies are to find true liberty, justice, and righteousness, the risen Christ must be part of that picture, right?"

I nodded again. He had taken me by the hand, and I knew where he was leading. I was powerless to do anything but follow.

"Then why in God's name are you unable to apply these truths to yourself? You load your shoulders with other people's sins, shortcomings, and inertias, yet you seem incapable of passing them on to the only One who knows how to handle them constructively. You come from the segment of the church that majors in salvation. So take that theology and apply it to yourself. As you do so, you will find release." I did what he said, and over the long haul, I have discovered that he was right.

Finding ways to keep the pastor physically, emotionally, and spiritually healthy should be high on the priority of the lay leadership of a congregation. It would be wise to build the cost of this into parish budgets—whether it be counseling or reshaping schedules so that the pastor can spend time with his family. The help Rachel and I received cost thousands of dollars. Without the support of our bishop, we would still be paying those debts today. Others are not so fortunate.

In the wake of my collapse, I have become more tolerant of

131

the failure of others—particularly ministers. I have a hunch that this is symptomatic of my evolving, altering spirituality. While I do not think the core of my theology has changed radically, my perspective has. With this realization has come the recognition that I cannot do it on my own.

Before all this happened I had the idea that I was invincible. I have been defeated once, but life dictates that I must sally forth daily onto the field of battle. Furthermore, my gut tells me I cannot do it alone. I must go with the Savior walking ahead of me and with loving friends supporting me from behind, allowing me to cry on their shoulders and enabling me to take on challenges from which I would rather run away. I need that kind of support because, to change the analogy, I have some bumps in my fenders and the gears don't shift as smoothly as they once could.

Until my crisis, my life was bound up in *doing*. My ambition was to achieve something spectacular for the Lord. So I rushed hither and yon, attempting to pull this "miracle" off. I have chronicled some of the results of those frenetic years of drivenness for you. While I remain an activist, I am learning now what it truly means to *be:* to be forgiven, for example.

As I come to terms with my own forgivenness, I am discovering that it is not so difficult to forgive others. Failure is a product of the human condition, and, if God is able to reclaim me, then he can reach down and pull any number of other unfortunates out of the mire. When you have hung over the abyss yourself, it is easier, far easier, to empathize with those who have had the misfortune to plunge into the boiling vat of misery.

I wish this dimension could have grown within me some other way. I have been judge and jury of many a weary traveler on the road of life who has not measured up to my expectations. Such intolerant self-righteousness has not been totally crushed underfoot yet. On a number of occasions during the last few years, when I have written someone off with some well-chosen words, I have heard my conscience mutter, "Haven't you got it yet?"

Like other Christian Pharisees, I am adept at making mincemeat of someone who does not measure up to *my* expectations. We who are part of the forgiven community of faith are called to be a forgiving community as well. A pastor who fails is rarely given the benefit of a doubt; yet those who try him seldom give thought to the fact that his experience of brokenness may ultimately turn someone rather ordinary into a genuine "wounded healer."

Epilogue

Jonathan glanced at his watch, and I knew our time was almost up. I looked around the room; metaphorically speaking, I had spilled a lot of blood within these four walls. As a result, my life was taking a different, better course.

The picture still hung there before me, the fields stretching away into the distance, the pathway beckoning me to follow it beyond the woods and out into the wide, wide world.

"Yes," I thought to myself, "I'm sure I will find the ocean beyond the trees—eventually."

Silence reigned. Neither of us quite knew how to terminate the session and return to being two ministers who meet occasionally at ecclesiastical functions. Later I would shed tears, but they would be tears of joy, tokens of health and restoration.

"Well, that's it," one of us said at last. It was the cue to rise and embrace.

"The peace of the Lord be always with you," Jonathan said, falling back into the comforting words of the liturgy.

"And also with you," I replied. I had used these words so many times in church, but today they took on a new meaning and fresh significance.

Jonathan came to the door of the counseling center with me, we embraced again, and then he was gone—back to embroil himself in the life of another client, another person desperately in need of mental health and inner peace. I slid into the driver's seat, turned on the engine, and headed out into the traffic.

I had crossed a Rubicon and was heading out on the first day of the rest of my life. By my side would be Rachel. How

135

foolish I had been ever to doubt her love for me and mine for her. Our children had come through the crisis relatively unscarred. I am now exercising a different kind of ministry, but one for which I feel eminently suited.

A few days later the mail carrier delivered a card with a Falmouth, Massachusetts, postmark. Not long before, Bishop Rees had retired and settled in that little town intent on tending his roses, writing his memoirs, and enjoying several rounds of golf each week. I had written him as soon as I got home from Jonathan's office to tell him that we had reached the end of the counseling process.

The bishop too felt it appropriate to respond to this news liturgically: "Thanks be to God. Go forth into the world rejoicing in the power of the Spirit!"

Appendix 1
Questions and Answers
About Burnout

Having read this story, perhaps you are wondering, "How do I know if I am heading for career burnout? What is the difference between the normal ups and downs of life and symptoms that should be taken more seriously?"

While a brief appendix cannot deal with every facet of your perplexity, here is a checklist that might help you understand burnout. A word of caution: The symptoms of burnout differ with the individual. While there are certain definable patterns, it is not a disease, the course of which can be diagnosed like chicken pox.

If you are spiritually and emotionally fit, then store the information away. The day may come when you need it. None of us has any idea what the future holds. Read other books on this phenomenon (see appendix 2).

A. Who are the top candidates for burnout?

Usually the *high achievers*. They tend to work hard, be creative, and have a strong—perhaps too strong—drive to succeed. They are the men and women who have the potential to make a significant contribution in their field.

Elijah is an example of a ministering person who burned out (1 Kings 18–19). Having been hounded unmercifully and having reached deep within himself to uphold the name of the Lord on Mount Carmel, he came to the point where he could take no more. Jezebel threatened and Elijah ran. Following his collapse, it took several months of rest, a healthy diet, and spiritual "reconstruction" to recommission him for service. Yet when he reappeared, his style had been altered and his ministry became significantly different than it previously had been.

History is littered with burnouts. Some have recovered and have gone on to make a significant impact; others have never been heard from again. The burned-out person joins the company of a host of outstanding individuals: St. Augustine of Hippo, Dante, Beethoven, Shakespeare, and possibly a certain Saul of Tarsus, to name just a few.

Some of the greatest creative thinkers burned out in midlife, a factor that probably contributed to their premature deaths: Mozart, Chopin, and F. Scott Fitzgerald, for example. Others weathered the storm. Shakespeare used the experience to enhance his maturity so that his later plays exhibit a depth absent from the feisty, earlier ones.

People often fail to see that the pastor is a creator. He or she creates structures of nurture, teaching, meaningful worship, and responsible care. The effect of such efforts is often unappreciated by clergy or their congregations. Thus it is a shock when clergy discover that they have drained their spiritual and emotional resources and are no longer fit for ministry.

Add to this the fact that "the ministering person cannot always tell if his work is having any results."[1] For a creator this can be a terrible indictment. No wonder so many older clergy appear beaten.

B. Why do pastors burn out?

1. *Overwork.* Most clergy work too hard, relax too little, and spend far too much time trying to live up to the expectations of their congregations. What is more, I am convinced that the job is getting harder.

Lyle Schaller writes:

---

[1] John A. Sanford, *Ministerial Burnout* (New York: Paulist Press, 1983), p. 22.

A score of changes . . . have enhanced the complexity of parish life and increased the difficulties facing the average congregational leader, either lay or clergy, in today's world. In more precise terms, it is more difficult today for a minister with an average level of skill and competence to be a happy and effective parish pastor than it was in the 1950s.[2]

2. *Too little recreation.* Jeremy Wilkinson was a man who chose not to go on vacation with his family. Like most clergy, he had a high sense of duty and felt that he would be not only shortchanging the congregation, but also incurring the wrath of his detractors if he took too much time off. So he labored on—and look what it did to him!

Most clergy work a six-day week and usually sneak in a chore or two on their "day off." Some, and I plead guilty to this sin, often ignore their need for a day off and just keep going. Not only is this a denial of the Creation ordinance, it is also plain stupidity.

Clergy are *never* able to get away for weekends with their families and are expected to be "on call" twenty-four hours a day. Recently, a Presbyterian friend of mine resigned from his parish in order to take a denominational task. He and his wife are echoing our conversations of several years ago: "How do you use this thing called 'a weekend'?"

3. *Loneliness.* Many clergy are some of the loneliest people I have come across. As far as the parish is concerned, they live in a "goldfish bowl," and sometimes it is very difficult to make close, supportive friendships. Others have little in common, either socially or intellectually, with the people among whom they minister.

Their fellow clergy are not always helpful. There are still far too many clergy gatherings where we compete against each other. Emphasis is placed on who has the biggest congregation, budget, youth group, Sunday school, etc. Instead of being an encouragement, such meetings can drain the energy from a pastor, particularly one going through a

[2] Lyle A. Schaller, *It's a Different World* (Nashville: Abingdon Press, 1987), p. 18.

bad patch or working in an "unrewarding" corner of the Lord's vineyard.

4. *Expectation Versus Reality.* Most men and women who enter the pastorate have high ideals. Like Jeremy Wilkinson, they give of themselves unstintingly in the service of the gospel. For many it comes as a rude shock to discover that the church has as many blemishes as any other human organization.

It is extremely draining to coax a congregation forward; and like the fictional St. Mary's in our story, there are some parishes that do not want the sort of ministry their leader has to offer. The result is that pastors find their expectations stymied and strip their gears as they come to grips with that reality.

But there are also the expectations that a congregation lays on its clergy. Not only do Christians sometimes send the message to their pastor that they want him to work until he drops, some also expect perfection in his family life and from his children. The reality is always different. While the pastor's family is a model to the congregation, it is the manner in which they solve the difficulties arising from their own imperfections that is probably the most important facet of this aspect of ministry.

5. *Frustration.* This arises from a pastor's encounters with the realities of parish life. A parish can be a stew pot of problems all looking for *immediate* resolution. There is also a dreadful sense among many clergy that their vocation has placed them on the periphery of society. Although they might be handling the congregation okay, they have a horrible feeling that they will not leave the world a better place.

It is frustrating to have a growing family and not have enough time to nurture them. In addition, some are asked to make ends meet on an impossibly low salary.

Then there are the frustrations caused by the combativeness of church politics, the inability to relocate rapidly out of a difficult situation, the lack of support from fellow clergy, bishops, or judicatory executives. The list is endless and can be tailored to suit each pastor's situation.

One writer puts the problem of the effects of frustration this way: "It seems to take only one precipitating event to push a pastor into despair."[3] For Jeremy Wilkinson, that event was the little fender-bender he had during Boston's evening rush hour. From there everything went downhill.

6. *Guilt:* Why guilt? Clergy are generally highly conscientious people. They have committed to pouring themselves out in the service of the Master; therefore they want to do their job exceptionally well. They desire to love and care for the parish as Christ would and inevitably fail to meet the standards they set for themselves.

Add to this the weight of listening to and identifying with the sins of failures of individuals in the congregation, often having no one with whom to share the secrets of the confessional. A process of transference readily takes place, and before you know it, they are trying to redeem their parishioners from their sins.

Guilt is part of the human condition, but it is a particularly powerful symptom of the pastoral condition. Without proper attention, it can crush and destroy.

7. *Too few hobbies and avocations.* My bishop is one of the healthiest people I know. Aside from his family and his ministry, his great passion is what he calls "the game"—golf. It is fun to play with him because he enjoys it so much, for it is also how he relaxes and unwinds.

Only in recent years have I begun to develop hobbies and interests aside from my work. I do not think I am unusual among clergy. Ministry is an incredibly time-consuming task, gobbling up not just our hours, but also emotional energy. In the ordained life not only does "all work and no play make Jack a dull boy," it is also likely to be part of the self-destructive cycle that eventually destroys him.

8. *Choked spirituality.* A symptom of Jeremy Wilkinson's dilemma was the breakdown of his devotional discipline and the onset of the "dark night of the soul." The latter may not

---

[3] G. Lloyd Rediger, *Coping with Clergy Burnout* (Valley Forge, Pa.: Judson Press, 1982), p. 41.

have been avoidable, but its destructive impact might have been reduced had he managed to keep his spiritual life a little fresher.

I know no easy answers to this problem. Most of us find the disciplines of prayer and Bible reading difficult. Sometimes we need to try a radically different approach to this aspect of our lives if we are to keep "the monsters" at bay.

9. *Midlife transition.* Midlife is probably a more upsetting time for many people than adolescence. As a teenager you have your whole life before you and are still collecting the colors with which to paint your canvas. By the late thirties or early forties your allotted span is possibly more than half over, and you know it.

You begin to see unfulfilled ambitions as bleak mountains you will never climb. The options before you are ever more limited, and you can only wistfully ponder facets of life ignored or overlooked. Many men yearn after a fresh intimacy; women who have been raising a family wonder about the possibilities of a new career.

Midlife is a time when many of us put our marriage under scrutiny. The wedding is ancient history, our offspring are demanding, our spouse is nowhere near as exciting as (s)he used to be, and we probably give too little time to each other.

Men, having worked like slaves, realize they want something more from their wives than they have asked. If she does not pick up his signals that she must do more to be a loving partner and intimate friend, the temptation might be overwhelming.

Like most men, Jeremy Wilkinson yearned for intimacy and found it in an attractive woman whose life had come unraveled. There is hardly a pastor or priest who has been ordained a few years who has not faced this particular struggle and temptation. Some of us handle it better than others. With the increase of divorced people in our parishes, this problem is not one that is going to go away in years to come.

10. *Relentlessly demanding congregations.* I am convinced that few congregations realize when they ask too much of their

clergy. Some have the kind of group personality that will gobble a pastor up, deny him a private life, and then spit him out when he is used up, without recognizing what they are doing.

Unfortunately, given the sort of people clergy are, many play into the hands of such parishes or groups of people within them. Clergy are not slaves—a lesson some of us still have to learn. It is imperative that sensitive persons in congregations keep an eye open to see whether their pastor is being given enough "space."

Summary. All told, like others in the caring professions, clergy spend so much time looking out for others that they are extremely bad at looking after themselves. Jeremy Wilkinson is a fine example of this and stands as a warning to and an indictment of a system that judges pastors on the basis of what they do rather than who they are.

An Episcopal priest whose marriage was crumbling once said to me, "The church rightly glorifies the family and the home and then promptly creates a system that is designed to destroy the domestic tranquility of its ordained servants and active lay leaders." The compulsive ministers among us play into the hands of such a system rather than challenging and altering it.

C. Can burnout be prevented?

In some cases probably not. With hindsight I can see that the damage done by my burning out could have been "contained," but it is unlikely that I could have avoided a significant trauma at that point in my life. My burnout was a complicated mixture of overwork and a difficult transition into middle age.

In retrospect, I believe that the Lord took an experience of failure and used it to teach me lessons about his love and grace. The first title I used when I began this book was "After Death Comes Resurrection"—these words so clearly told my story.

Through burnout I discovered that my energy was not infinite and that my judgment can be badly flawed. I crumpled up in a heap on the ground, but God picked me up, dusted me off, and after my recuperation, sent me on my way rejoicing.

While saying this about myself, it is not true of everyone. I am convinced that pastors, their families, congregations, and leaders can prevent some of the negative effects that arise out of such chapters in their lives. The suggestions I make below are ones that I have learned after the fact. I wish I had heeded them before it!

1. *Know yourself.* Know your strengths, weaknesses, and limitations. Be honest with yourself and with God. Most of us overdo it, laying on the altar our physical and mental health, our families, and ultimately our ministries. Make use of colleagues, counselors, "soul friends," and family members so that you realize your limitations and live within them.

As I get older, I become ever more convinced that every pastor needs as spiritual director someone able to help him or her in the pilgrimage of life, someone who might be able to wave a red flag before problems have deteriorated too far. Only by letting an outsider into your life will you learn to see yourself as others and God might see you. In such a setting it is possible to learn the lessons of grace.

2. *Do not try to bypass doubts and difficulties.* To give priority to my ministry, I shelved my marriage and put faith-related problems on the back burner. My doubts came back and chewed out my spiritual and intellectual innards like a pack of hungry rats.

Like Jeremy Wilkinson, I reached a point of temporary unbelief. While this forced me to carefully reassess the foundation upon which I had built my life, it would not have been so hard nor have caused such pain to my congregation if I had dealt with festering issues earlier.

Mine was not a case of "terminal doubt."[4] But under the stress of abject personal failure, I learned how fragile it really

---

[4] Os Guinness, *In Two Minds* (Downers Grove, Ill.: InterVarsity Press, 1977), p. 237.

was and how dependent I am upon the loving-kindness of a merciful God.

3. *Take care of your marriage.* During the time I was going under, my spouse and I were not looking out for our relationship. She was too busy raising the children, and I was too busy being a parish priest. When things got out of hand, our marriage spiraled downward, and we were forced to deal with problems we had conveniently sublimated.

My wife and I fought viciously, dealing with the backlog of bitterness that had been piling up like dirty dishes in the kitchen sink. In counseling, we spent many hours putting ourselves and our marriage back together again. Today, despite demanding schedules, we attempt to give ourselves quality time together.

With our children that much older, it is easier to get time on our own. But the work that I now do is more demanding than the ministry that brought me to my emotional knees, so carving out that time can be hard work. The only way we could do it last week was to buy some fast food and sit in the sunshine near my wife's office.

4. *Find a support group.* During the years leading up to my own collapse, unlike Jeremy Wilkinson, I was part of several small groups of fellow pastors. I found them encouraging and helpful, but unfortunately, whenever we started becoming a little community of support, some would move away, and I would be forced to start over. Had these groups remained intact, I would have had a stronger safety net.

If you are not part of a small group already, go out and find some like-minded individuals who would like to share a sandwich, Bible study, prayer, discussion, etc. Out of such gatherings come lifelong friendships and a whole gamut of creative ideas.

5. *Take vacations and sabbaticals.* I write this a few days after returning from two weeks' vacation. Despite all we have gone through, my wife still had to drag me away from my ministry. I am so glad she did, because I am facing some demanding problems in the next few months, and now I feel refreshed and ready to take them on.

145

Congregations should build into their pastor's package adequate vacation and study leave; and having done that, they should insist that the time is used. Too many parishioners lay a guilt trip on the pastor so that he feels bad about going away. Every effort should be made to make him feel uncomfortable about *not* going away!

For a creative person, a sabbatical is an essential. The preacher-teacher must have blocks of uninterrupted time every few years to go away to read, think, meditate, and recharge intellectual and spiritual batteries. A pastor who is doing the job properly needs a sabbatical just as much, if not more, than a college professor or school teacher.

6. *Pastoring within denominational structures.* Whatever their original intention, many denominational structures do not allow for the pastoral care of clergy. In fact, some judicatories seem designed to destroy rather than build up ministering persons.

Two of the pastors whose real-life situation helped create the person of Jeremy Wilkinson were as much victims of the ecclesiastical system as of their own exhaustion, failure, or foolishness. Both are gifted and sensitive men; neither is in ministry today, and I believe one has dropped out of church life altogether.

I was fortunate. I have a bishop who is a pastor and who took the time to love and care for me. Sometimes his love was tough, and there were occasions when he expected me to obey him, but he shepherded us through a long, dark tunnel. He is not perfect, but he saved my ministry, and for that I am eternally grateful.

Judicatory executives have a profound responsibility to love their clergy through crises, not merely to shuffle papers. I like to think of my bishop as my priest, confessor, pastor, and friend. I wish that others in crisis had such support.

D. What can laypeople do?

1. *Affirm your pastor.* While there are many elements of the pastoral task that are enjoyable, fulfilling, and wonderfully affirming, the pastor is often the scapegoat for anything that

goes wrong at church. You may not believe it, but however careful the pastor has been, there is always someone in the parish over whose toes (s)he has unwittingly walked. Troublesome relationships are one of the most draining elements of pastoral ministry.

Affirming the pastor means more than saying, "That was a fine sermon," as you shake hands at the church door. It involves acts of kindness; hugs; statements of affirmation; adequate support in the ministry; and at the very least, your friendship.

I burned out after a long period during which I received little affirmation and a great number of kicks. Some I deserved, but many were unnecessary. Only since leaving that congregation have I learned how much my ministry and our family were appreciated by a majority of the parish.

2. *Make sure that your pastor has adequate time for refreshment.* A few years ago a close friend of mine came through a series of very tough problems. The congregation saw that he was at his wit's end. With the help of their judicatory executive, they arranged a three-month sabbatical for their pastor at extremely short notice.

The time away was the tonic he and his family needed. After his return, the parish experienced some of their most fruitful years. Such caring affirmation paid off for everyone concerned. Sabbaticals, study leaves, retreats, and vacations are a must if a minister is to do a worthwhile job.

3. *Make sure that your pastor is properly paid.* By and large, clergy are better paid than in the past, but it is surprising how many congregations keep their pastors in penury. Most people who get ordained know that they are unlikely to get rich, but it plays havoc with a minister's nerves to be not only relatively poor in relation to his parishioners, but also to have the bills piling up.

Add to this the inevitable education debts and perhaps a significant drop in standard of living for those who have come into ordained ministry from another career, and a parish can find itself being led by a very troubled person. Such financial stress can be debilitating.

4. *But what if the minister has burned out already?* First of all, treat the pastor and his or her family with tender, loving care no matter what (s)he might have done that has caused pain or embarrassment. A congregation is in a position to make or break a servant of God at this point. Denominational leaders must be involved at this stage, and they too ought to be gentle rather than heavy-handed with the victim.

Rob bailed out of his ministry by getting involved with another woman. He left his wife and moved in with the other woman. There was no question that he had effectively terminated his ministry in that parish and city. Had the denominational executive and the congregation's leaders been a little more generous, Rob and his former wife might possibly have been able to rebuild something. It has been a long, hard road back for that man.

Heavy-handedness is the natural reaction because Christians feel betrayed when their leaders fail, but generosity often brings redemption. Remember what Jesus said: "Let him who is without sin throw the first stone."

Appendix 2
Resources to Deal With Burnout

In this section you will find resources to assist in the understanding and treatment of burnout. While my emphasis is on clergy, much of the information can be used by people of every background. Career burnout can affect anyone in any profession, but ministerial burnout often cripples lay leaders juggling business and church responsibilities.

I hope you will find these resources helpful as you acquaint yourself with the topic. If I had had a better understanding of what burnout entails, perhaps my family, congregation, and I, myself, would not have been so badly bruised. This list is not exhaustive. What I have outlined are materials that have helped me and others with whom I have talked.

Counseling

While thousands have recovered from burnout without the help of a counselor, the process can be speeded up and made a "learning experience" if the victim and his or her family put themselves in the hands of a professional therapist.

My experience enabled me to deal with inadequacies in my personality that I probably would not have looked at had there not been another party asking the probing questions and forcing me to dig deeply into my heart and soul.

The person called "Jonathan" is modeled on my therapist, a friend who has spent many years in this field. The counselor who helped me approaches the Christian faith from a slightly different perspective than I do, but he never attempt to impose his distinctive point of view on me when I was vulnerable.

In addition, antidepressant drugs were used in my healing process. The psychiatrist who prescribed them and monitored my progress was extraordinarily helpful. Even though I am ambivalent about the long-term value of drug therapy, it definitely figured in bringing me back from the edge of the abyss.

Members of the helping professions are always the last to seek therapy, for their pride often prevents them from recognizing their own needs. As a result of my experience, I have come to realize that far from using a therapist at a time of crisis, ministering people need an ongoing relationship with a person who can help monitor their psychological health in relation to the other stresses on their lives. This person need not be a trained therapist. All of us probably need a spiritual director who can fill this role and best recognize when our psyche is so battered that a professional should be drawn in.

If you do not know whom to approach for counseling, speak to other clergy. Most ministers I know have a good idea of the effective therapists in the area, especially those likely to be most sensitive to the special needs of ministering persons.

Books on Burnout

Freudenberger, Herbert J. *Burnout.* New York: Anchor Press, 1980.

This book is also available in paperback from Bantam. It is a popular how-to publication. The author is similar to so many clergy in his compulsiveness about his work. From the dark abyss of the experience of burnout came this fine piece of work. Although it is not written specifically with the church in mind, I heartily recommend it.

Grider, Edgar M. *Can I Make It One More Year?* Atlanta: John Knox Press, 1980.

The thread running through this volume is that anxiety, if it is properly handled, can be a creative adjunct to ministry and not something that will distract from one's effectiveness. This is heavy reading, but it is worth wrestling with because it has much to offer.

Hart, Archibald D. *Coping With Depression in the Ministry and Other Caring Professions*. Waco, Tex.: Word Books, 1984.

This is a fairly technical volume that I have found helpful as I have sought to understand my own depressive tendencies and the part that these played in my burnout. Dean of the School of Psychology at Fuller Seminary, Pasadena, California, Dr. Hart has a profound message for clergy in crisis.

Hulme, William E. *Managing Stress in Ministry*. San Francisco: Harper and Row, 1985.

Written by the professor of pastoral care and pastoral counseling at Luther Northwestern Seminary, St. Paul, Minnesota, this book is a practical handbook that identifies and addresses the stress factors that are at the root of so much ministerial burnout.

Rassieur, Charles L. *Christian Renewal—Living Beyond Burnout*. Philadelphia: Westminster Press, 1984.

This book, after a brief summary of the causes of stress, gives a thorough roll call of the actions that need to be taken to prevent burnout from happening or to recreate your life after burnout. The message that comes loud and clear through every page is that God enters our despair and transforms it.

Rediger, G. Lloyd. *Coping With Clergy Burnout*. Valley Forge, Pa.: Judson Press, 1982.

G. Lloyd Rediger is director of the Office of Pastoral Services for the Wisconsin Council of Churches. Interspersed with case studies are thorough lists of causes and symptoms. More systematic than Sanford, this book makes an excellent reference tool.

Sanford, John A. *Ministry Burnout*. New York: Paulist Press, 1982.

John Sanford is an Episcopal priest, writer, and therapist. I have found this the clearest and most practical of any book I have read on this subject. Particularly helpful are the suggestions on how to avoid burnout that he spells out in the last chapter.

Slaikeu, Karl, and Steve Lawhead. *The Phoenix Factor*. Boston: Houghton Mifflin, 1985.

————. *Up From the Ashes*. Grand Rapids: Zondervan, 1987.

These two delightfully well-written handbooks, covering essentially the same territory on surviving and growing through the experience of personal crisis, can readily be applied to the problem of ministerial burnout. The thesis is that out of the ashes of the past a new life can arise. They plot the anatomy of a personal crisis and assist the reader to find ways through it and forward to greater creativity. *The Phoenix Factor* is addressed to the secular market. *Up From the Ashes* is written with Christians in mind. Karl Slaikeu is an adjunct seminary professor.

The Alban Institute

For pastors and congregations, the Alban Institute in Washington, D.C., is probably one of the most significant resources available to clergy who experience burnout. The institute researches the dynamics of congregational and clergy life and develops conferences and other events to enable Christians to deal with the variety of crises that afflict their lives, individually or in community.

The Alban Institute is directed by the Reverend Loren Mead, an Episcopal priest. It is an ecumenical, nonprofit foundation with membership dues at various levels. It publishes a quarterly journal.

I have much appreciated their publications and have found the institute's materials dealing with everything from the clergy family to church fights an extremely important resource.

> The Alban Institute
> 4125 Nebraska Avenue, N.W.
> Washington, D.C. 20016
> (202) 244–7320

Retreats

Sometimes it is important for the burned-out pastor to get into a caring, communal environment where he can receive the nurture he or she needs. Recovery does not come "out of the blue," and for centuries religious orders and retreat houses have provided hospitality to the hurting and spiritually exhausted.

Throughout the country there are convents and monasteries that welcome visitors for a while. Some are Roman Catholic and others are Episcopal or Orthodox. The members of most orders are eager to assist their guests in their struggles.

I recently learned of *St. Raphael's House, Evergreen, Colorado.* Set high in the mountains about twenty-five miles northwest of Denver, there is a commuter bus service in and out of the city. The house is run by the Community of St. Mary, an Episcopal order of sisters. There is a small chapel in which the community and visitors worship, and they have rooms for eight pastors and their spouses. They have set up their retreat house with the needs of clergy in mind, especially those requiring an extended period of rehabilitation.

> St. Raphael's House
> P.O. Box 43
> Evergreen, CO 80439
> (303) 674–4179

Books on Related Topics

Berkley, Jim. *Making the Most of Your Mistakes.* Waco, Tex.: Word/CTI, 1987.

Using the case-study, easy-reading style of *Leadership,* the associate editor of that publication explores the stories of a number of individuals who have used their mistakes as a springboard for growth and renewed ministry.

Bolles, Richard Nelson. *What Color Is Your Parachute?* Berkeley, Calif.: Ten Speed Press, updated annually.

This book, written by a pastor, includes appendices listing career guidance resources for clergy and places to go to get assistance with career burnout.

Brewi, Janice, and Anne Brennan. *Midlife: Psychological and Spiritual Perspectives.* New York: Crossroad Publishing, 1985.

Provocative and thoughtful study of midlife by two Roman Catholic sisters.

153

Conway, Jim. *Men in Midlife Crisis*. Elgin, Ill.: David C. Cook, 1981.

Midlife was a traumatic experience for this Midwestern evangelical pastor.. Here he pulls out of his experience the issues with which men must wrestle at midlife. Distilled wisdom, engagingly written.

Dittes, James. *When Work Goes Sour*. Philadelphia: Westminster Press, 1987.

A wonderful book describing the plight of men who have "love affairs" with their careers.

Levinson, Daniel J. *Seasons of a Man's Life*. New York: Ballantine Books, 1978.

A well-researched study of the developmental progress of men. Helpful to women, but their maturation follows a slightly different pattern than males.

Mace, David, and Vera Mace. *What's Happening to Clergy Marriages?* Nashville: Abingdon Press, 1983.

Burnout and marital problems are closely related. The Maces have spent many years working with pastors and spouses as they wrestle with home and ministry. Highly recommended.

Peterson, Eugene H. *Working the Angles*. Grand Rapids: Eerdmans, 1987.

I have long admired and learned much from Eugene Peterson's approach to ministry. In this publication he challenges the workaholic approach to parish life, asking clergy to consider their vocation to prayer, the Word, and spiritual direction.

Sheehy, Gail. *Passages*. New York: Bantam Books, 1976.

A runaway best seller written following the author's midlife emotional collapse. Journalistic in style, it is accessible to most readers.